PRAISE FOR **MINE'S BIGGER THAN YOURS**

"An innovative and informative perspective on one of the most talked-about but least ur of leadership. This book tells you all about the ego and how it is used to negative effect in organizations. Rea valuable insights that will help them business and personal lives."
Martin Gammon, Director, OCS

"This accessible and thoughtful book builds the business case for ego-free leadership and provides a how-to guide to help today's leaders demonstrate greater humility, integrity and self-awareness in all that they do."
Dr Paul Brewerton, Managing Director,
Blue Edge Consulting

"An important contribution to developing our ability to work effectively with our peers and create successful working environments."
Lesley Pugh, OD consultant, Creative Change Facilitation

"This isn't a book for the faint-hearted. If you want a clear route map to effective leadership development and an understanding of what that involves and why it is so valuable in an ever-competitive globalized market, then this may be the book for you. It mixes clarity about the journey with descriptions of effective leadership in action and challenging exercises for readers to use in their own learning."
Janine Clarke, Head of People Management,
Barts and the London Hospital

"Illuminates in a highly readable and practical way the consequences of ego-driven behaviours in the workplace, and through examples from organizational life and reflective exercises invites us to embody the potential we might become."
Professor Paul Barber, Work-based Learning,
Middlesex University

MINE'S BIGGER THAN YOURS

MINE'S BIGGER THAN YOURS

UNDERSTANDING & HANDLING EGOS AT WORK

SUSAN DEBNAM

Copyright © 2006 Susan Debnam

First published in 2006 by:

Marshall Cavendish Limited
119 Wardour Street
London W1F 0UW
United Kingdom
T: +44 (0)20 7565 6000
F: +44 (0)20 7734 6221
E: sales@marshallcavendish.co.uk
Online bookstore: www.marshallcavendish.co.uk

and

Cyan Communications Limited
119 Wardour Street
London W1F 0UW
United Kingdom
T: +44 (0)20 7565 6120
E: sales@cyanbooks.com
www.cyanbooks.com

A CIP record for this book is available from the
British Library

ISBN-13 978-1-904879-64-0
ISBN-10 1-904879-64-0

Printed and bound in Great Britain by
TJ International Ltd, Padstow, Cornwall

DEDICATION

This book is dedicated to my husband and daughter,
Joe and Sophie Booth. For their love and inspiration.

CONTENTS

ACKNOWLEDGMENTS

There are many people who have helped me with the creation of this book, taking it from a seed of an idea to a fully-formed manuscript.

I was delighted and honoured when Sally Bibb first invited me to submit a proposal to the publisher, Cyan, for the *The Truth About Business* series. The words 'support' and 'encouragement' do not do justice to all that Sally has given me over the past few months. I thank Sally for her inspiration, her generosity of spirit and her professionalism.

Writing a book takes time and energy in large quantities. I thank my husband and business partner Joe Booth for supporting me in taking the space to write, for his intelligent analysis and for knowing when to keep out of the way.

To Cressida and James I would like to say thank you for your interest and enthusiasm and for reminding me occasionally that it's pretty cool to write a book. When the going was tough, their lightness encouraged me to keep going.

For being inquisitive, for her unedited questions and her love of learning I want to acknowledge and honour my daughter, Sophie. She is an endless source of inspiration and I wish her a life of outrageous curiosity.

Without Martin, Pom and all the Cyan team this book may not have taken shape. I thank them for their professionalism, their interest and their integrity.

My gratitude goes to those people who have been invaluable in providing material for *Mine's Bigger Than Yours*. I send a sincere and humble thank you to my research participants for giving their time to tell me their stories. Their insight and honesty in recounting often difficult, sometimes hilarious experiences reinforced my view that this was a book worth writing.

I send warm thanks to Lesley. I deeply value her love and friendship. And I am inspired and energised by her ability to pick up on an idea and to have a discussion about anything, at any time, from a standing start. She always has something interesting and valuable to contribute to a debate. I know we will go on talking for ever.

INTRODUCTION

INTRODUCTION

Wherever you look you see egos at work. In business (most boardroom battles are about ego), politics, the media, the church, the armed forces or the local voluntary group. There will always be those who ask primarily "What's in it for me? How will I look? How will this action affect my career, my status, my credibility?"

Most of the time we ignore or accommodate the ego-driven boss, the controlling colleague. We learn how to "work" them, to lessen the impact of their seemingly irrational and often irritating behaviour. But what happens when someone else's needs – for power, status and recognition – get out of hand and begin to damage relationships, hamper productivity and infect the workplace culture? How do we identify ego-driven behaviour and what can we do about it? How do we know when we are working in an ego-infested culture and why should we be bothered?

Some of the most powerful leaders emerging globally are those who know what's in it for them, but are not driven by a need for glory. These are the men and women who have high levels of self-awareness and self-esteem, who will leave a legacy of success because they are big enough to nurture the strengths and acknowledge the needs of those around them. They are confident enough to promote the concept that glory is for everyone and doesn't have to die out when they move on. These leaders are not ego-less, but they are ego free. And in an increasingly competitive marketplace it is crucial to know the difference.

A VALUABLE INSIGHT

Looking through the ego lens will give you valuable insight into yourself, your colleagues and your business. It will help you understand what the ego is, how your own ego can get caught up in power games with those around you, what to do when other people's egos get out of hand and how to foster an ego-free culture.

Mine's Bigger Than Yours is not intended to be a quick fix. It does, I believe, offer a fascinating glimpse into what lies beneath the surface in many organisations. It will help you formulate a strategy for action, whether at the individual, group or strategic level of your business. I hope you enjoy it. And I hope you use it.

Let me know.

Susan Debnam
www.minesbiggerthanyours.co.uk

1

BIG EGO? WHY WORRY?

WHAT IS IT WITH EGOS?

What is it with egos? They have an inordinate capacity to make us laugh and cry, tear our hair out and collapse with exhaustion. One of the things you cannot do with an ego is ignore it. Egos crave attention and that's exactly what they set out to attract. One eminent professor of psychology said "think about it – one of the functions of the ego is to get you to notice them. You think about them all the time. You wake up thinking about them. You talk about them even after they've left. You tell stories about them in the pub. They are just there in your mind even when you're not with them. There is always a manifestation of the person with the big ego that goes way beyond their physical presence. They put down markers, like a cat leaving a scent".

Egos aren't intrinsically bad. Egos have drive and energy that can be infectious and, if used appropriately, can be highly productive. But they don't come with a user manual. When they reside in individuals or organisations that lack awareness of their impact they can wreak personal and corporate havoc. Having an ego isn't like having an illness. We don't get someone to pop a pill when we notice they're suffering from a bad bout of egotism. What we tend to do is shy away and wait for the storm to blow over. But how much more productive could our working lives be if we understood the workings of the ego and how to manage it in ourselves, our colleagues and more widely in the corporate culture?

ANTHONY

Anthony was charming, charismatic and powerful. A gifted entrepreneur he gathered round him the brightest minds and the most well-connected individuals to give his new media company the lift it needed to get it off the ground.

At first people were flattered by his invitations to support his venture. He offered not just financial reward but the promise of fame and prestige as his ideas began to flow and his plans began to take shape. He let it be known that he only worked with the best and that he expected their total commitment. Everyone acknowledged that in the early stages a new business needed a lot of hard work and dedication. They appreciated Anthony needed a sounding board to try out his ideas. They knew they needed to be flexible and accommodating while his new venture became established.

Anthony expected a lot from those around him. He expected them to be available. He expected them to work long hours to make his ideas a reality. He expected them to agree with him and support his ideas.

As the business grew it became apparent that Anthony could no longer take sole charge of the day-to-day running of an ever expanding enterprise. He needed to delegate. He appointed a client manager to lighten his workload. But somehow the time was never quite right to allow this client manager to go out and do what he had been tasked to do. Meet clients. Anthony was always there, watching, listening, taking a lead in the discussions.

Anthony was good at talking. A mellifluous orator he would spend hours preparing elaborate presentations that he would then spend even more hours delivering. He *knew* people needed to hear what he had to say. He had expertise and wisdom that *had* to be shared. The business would flounder without it. There was rarely time for questions, debate or challenge. So people took their doubts and their opinions away and aired them after work over a glass of wine.

As the business grew, Anthony's demands on his staff became more urgent and more frequent. He would call them at home late in the evening to tell them about an important new development or ask them to put in a couple of extra hours to work on a new initiative. He would fail to hear their requests to call him back when they had finished eating or working on an earlier request for a detailed report. He expected his requests to be dealt with immediately. After all, weren't these people getting well paid, as well as having the benefit of working with someone who could teach them everything?

Over time, commitment and enthusiasm amongst his team began to wane. They were physically exhausted by his demands and frustrated that their needs and opinions were given no space. What had been seen and indulged as Anthony's quirky behaviour came to irritate.

One or two of the more robust colleagues decided it was time to take Anthony aside and talk to him about his behaviour. They didn't want a fight they just wanted to explain how they felt and the impact his demands were having on their lives. After work one evening two of them took him to a wine bar to talk through their concerns. After a couple of minutes Anthony interrupted their flow.

He was angry. Outraged. Dismayed that they could be so disloyal, so blaming, when all he was trying to do was build a business that would benefit them all. Once again he launched into a well rehearsed tirade about what he was trying to achieve and why he needed 200% commitment from his staff.

The next day he apologised. The stress, he said, was getting to him. He needed a break, but of course that was impossible because without him the whole venture would fall apart. There could be no substitute for his expertise, his daily contact with high profile clients and backers. And while they were there, could he just talk them through a new idea that would need a bit of extra work over the next couple of weeks?

People began to regret that no contracts of employment had been signed. Anthony had lured them in with his promises but had never quite got round to putting any agreement in writing. Surely they were all friends and friends didn't need such formalities?

Anthony's behaviour with his team was echoed in his dealings with his clients. Over time they too tired of his speeches, his outbursts and his unwillingness to enter into debate or hear what they wanted. One by one they pulled out, frustrated and angry at his inability to recognise their needs.

People in the team were flagging. Anthony had taken over their lives. It seemed as though he was with them all the time. They talked about him when he wasn't there. They spent hours wondering what drove him and why he behaved the way he did. One of them said he had become the third person in his marriage and the strain was beginning to take its toll.

One by one the individuals Anthony had so carefully chosen fell away. Despite his desperate pleas and outlandish offers of more money, more responsibility, they left. All of them. Anthony was left with no clients and no team. How could they, he wondered, all be so stupid?

PROTECTING YOUR OWN EGO: A VALID LEADERSHIP OBJECTIVE?

If protecting your own ego were a valid leadership objective many current corporate and political leaders would be basking in the golden glow of achievement. We've become used to seeing big egos strutting their stuff, battling it out in the boardroom and on the world stage. If asked to think of five egotistical people right now, people known to us personally or those identified through the media, we would probably have little difficulty compiling the list. The word ego has slipped easily into current usage. It has become a shorthand for describing the narcissistic self-serving behaviours and qualities we experience in those who have power and influence over us at work and more broadly in society. Egocentricity has almost become something to be proud of. We are intrigued by and drawn towards big personalities, flamboyant characters.

ADMIRATION FOR CHARISMATIC LEADERS

We yearn to become charismatic leaders. Yet we hardly ever hear anyone speak with awe and admiration about the corporate leader who displays humility and authenticity.

Organisations have come to rely upon people with big, robust personalities, flamboyance and charisma. However, as we can see with Anthony, there is a cost, both to the individuals caught in the wake of these characters and to the interests of the organisations they work in if these charismatic qualities are not supported by fundamental self-awareness. Later on in this book we will explore in depth some of the costs and advantages of nurturing egocentric personalities and identify ways we can use the energy they bring and use that energy creatively.

Many of the leaders we describe as charismatic are narcissists by another name. Think of the high-powered, high-profile woman who is clearly working her own agenda and putting her own needs ahead of the business. Or the man who can deliver the most eloquent argument but is unable to listen or take in information he doesn't want to hear. Think of the colleague who likes to come across as tough, resilient, a laugh a minute, but who cannot tolerate dissent or criticism. Think of the most egocentric person you have ever encountered. And think of the emotions that person generates in almost everyone around him. Everything from outrage to indulgence. Outrage is perhaps the most understandable response. We are outraged because egocentric behaviour in others can leave us feeling inadequate, angry and powerless. We feel intimidated but completely incapable of taking any meaningful counter action. Sometimes it's even difficult to articulate our frustration. We become immobilised, temporarily unable to take an assertive stand. But the costs of doing nothing can be great, personally, professionally, financially and ethically.

INDULGENCE

Why the indulgent response? Why do we indulge these self-serving individuals? What is it about them that encourages us to tolerate and excuse their behaviour? Maybe we consider ourselves more mature, more stable, more worldly wise. Perhaps we see through the brash, brazen behaviour to the scared child within and consider ourselves above it all. Or perhaps we simply don't have the courage or confidence to take any action. When we see our boss, or a colleague, behaving egotistically we shrug and dismiss what we've seen rather than rock an already unstable boat.

Why do ego-driven individuals push our buttons? Clearly there is *something* about the egotistical boss that gets under our skin, drives us to behave in ways we wouldn't normally behave. There is *something* about the colleague with the big ego that makes us feel manipulated and frustrated. And we become incensed by the egos that play out on the international stage, criticising world leaders for creating cultures in which it is OK to preen and posture, vie for position and in the extreme invade each others' lands.

Every day we experience the fall-out from ego-driven behaviour. Sometimes that behaviour is so exaggerated that we don't need a degree in psychology to begin to identify what's going on. In the world of the egocentric, size really does matter. Big office, big car, big salary, big opinions, an armoury of electronic gadgets. When egotism manifests in manipulation or intimidation and we are on the receiving end we feel pain and anger. But sometimes the effects of ego-driven behaviour are more subtle and therefore harder to define and tackle. Take for instance competitive presenteeism: the boss that *has* to be in before everyone else and makes a point of leaving last. Or the gradual establishment of an "in-crowd/out-crowd culture" with colleagues who huddle together for safety, making light-hearted comments belittling others' contribution and values. We cringe at behaviour we describe as patronising but find it hard to put a label on it or do anything about it. Understanding that this destructive behaviour can be ego-driven is the first step in formulating a strategy for dealing with it.

EGOS AT WAR

A couple of years ago I was invited to design and run a mentoring programme for a group of directors with another consultant, someone I had never met. The day came to have the first in a series of pre-meetings to discuss the content and approach we would adopt when running the event. I booked a meeting room in central London and sat with my papers and a coffee thinking, anticipating, looking forward to a creative and productive morning. Derek swaggered in. Shoulders back. Chin forward. Scanning the room with his eyes, every foot fall carefully and deliberately placed to cover maximum space. I was stunned. Although at that moment I could not have articulated what was going on, it was as though a contest had begun that I didn't know I'd signed up for. I'm pretty assertive but in no more than 30 seconds I found I had gone from relaxed and curious to defensively alert. My energy and attention had been drawn away from the content of the programme we were supposed to be discussing to the dynamic that was unfolding between the two of us.

At the end of the meeting I felt exhausted, as though I had, quite literally, been in a battle. On reflection I realised that the battle that had been raging was between our two respective egos. Without acknowledging it openly we had both been vying for position, trying to gain the upper hand, proving our worth, posturing and preening. Statements were slipped into the conversation about the prestige of our respective client bases, the importance of our roles, the geographical breadth of our fantastically important work that would ultimately lead to world peace and everlasting harmony... Whoa! Who was in charge here? Us or our egos?

If they could have sat down together later over a drink in the bar what might those two egos have said about that meeting?

"We got 'em running around that time didn't we?"

"Yes! Did you notice when mine tensed up and went all red in the face and made that comment about being known as the most awesome consultant his clients had ever known?"

"I know, I know! Then she went all supercilious and said something about the quality and value of what she did and how clients always came back for more..."

"And it was all said *so* casually and *so* politely as though it wasn't really important."

"You know what though?"

"What?"

"They think they do all this clever stuff but when it comes down to it we're the ones in charge..."

"Absolutely mate. Absolutely."

DO WE LAUGH, CRY OR COUNT THE COST?

It's often easier to pretend to be amused by appalling ego-driven behaviour than it is to do anything about it. We shrug it off. We laugh indulgently as a parent does when it sees a wayward toddler stamping its foot or acting up to get attention. Somehow it's easier to give way to the small petulant child inside the big ego-driven adult than it is to take a stand. But what happens if we don't take a stand? What havoc and destruction unfolds when we do nothing? How does tolerance and inactivity in the face of a big ego impact on us, our colleagues, the business, the corporate culture and beyond?

Many of us will have laughed, cringed and identified with the scenes played out in the BBC's *The Office*. Ricky Gervais, in creating the David Brent character, exquisitely described some of the uncertainty, the anger, the confusion and demotivation, the loss of productivity that can ensue when an unchecked ego is on the rampage. David Brent, the office manager at Wernham Hoggs, lacked any self-awareness or sensitivity to the needs of those around him, or indeed any obvious leadership qualities. We, the viewers, watched with awe and horror as the character unfolded as a deluded, self-centred individual who was quite unable to see any situation other than in relation to himself. He was quite clearly the centre of his own universe. His need for attention, approval and power was played out in every scene, every interaction with his staff. At no point did he set himself and his own needs aside for the greater good of the team, the business, or any individual within it. And yet we laughed. Probably because we could either identify personally with some of the Brent traits, or because we had seen them acted out for real in our workplaces. There, in front of our eyes, was a portrayal of our deepest, darkest, hidden selves, our shadow sides that we struggle to admit to in ourselves, but will happily attribute to a larger than life caricature that becomes a scapegoat or a dumping ground for all the bits of ourselves that we don't like.

THE PRICE TAG

Of course it's wonderful to be able to laugh at the Brents of the world, whether fictional characters or real-life individuals that we bump into every day of our working lives. But there has to be a cost attached to egocentricity. In corporate life at least we seem to be addicted to measuring, pricing, costing. We want value for money, we strive to meet targets, measure outputs, analyse inputs. If it moves or stands still we want to know the value of its contribution and if it's not adding value, we ditch it. Yet no-one has ever thought to put a price tag on one of the most powerful, influential and potentially destructive forces that drives its way through corporate and political life: the ego.

What *are* the costs of ego-driven behaviour, to individuals, to teams, to businesses, to productivity? Who and what suffers? And how? Later in the book we will examine these questions in some detail and look at what can be done to counter some of the negative effects. For now let's identify some of the more undesirable manifestations of an inflated ego allowed to reign supreme. Have you experienced any of the following in your workplace?

UNDESIRABLE EFFECTS OF AN INFLATED EGO

- intimidation
- bullying
- greed
- pride
- individual and collective loss of confidence
- culture of fear and manipulation
- no-one prepared to take risks
- opportunities to learn are missed
- low productivity
- individuals "kept in their place"
- culture of dishonesty
- fear of giving and receiving honest feedback
- stifling of creativity
- loss of good people
- haemorrhaging of intellectual capital

It may be difficult to cost these precisely, but unless decision makers in organisations acknowledge that there *is* a cost attached to these ego-driven manifestations they will suffer the consequences indefinitely. We don't always think about these behaviours as being ego-driven, but looking through the ego lens can help us understand what's going on and why. Of course there may be other root causes behind these individual symptoms but it's likely that if you look behind any of them you will be able to trace a line back to an inflated, or a fragile ego – and the two can look remarkably similar – lurking somewhere in the system or organisation.

A CORPORATE CULTURAL ISSUE THAT SOMEONE NEEDS TO OWN AND TACKLE

The ego is a very powerful force and yet it is ignored, downplayed, tolerated. Perhaps we have become so accustomed to the negative fall out of the inflated ego that we no longer recognise its impact. We have all come across people who:

- ask only "what's in it for me?"
- know our vulnerabilities and push our buttons
- crave attention
- intimidate and manipulate
- bully
- seek approval
- display envy, jealousy, greed, desire, lust, hatred, anger, pride, self-centredness
- talk endlessly about themselves
- pay no attention to others views or needs
- think they are the best and believe others should treat them with unconditional respect

These people are addicted to power and status. Often the addiction is so deeply embedded that they don't realise it's there. But it *is* there and they will do all they can to feed that addiction, no matter what the cost to those around them or to the business. Maybe we can forgive, or even feel sympathy for the individual who, lacking self-awareness and emotional intelligence, carries on doing what he's always done and gets the same old responses from those around him. If it serves him well and keeps his ego intact, why change? But can we afford to tolerate the disturbing lack of corporate awareness of the impact of this behaviour? What impact are these inflated or fragile egos having on business success? Shareholders be worried. Organisations are scared and ignorant. They will pour endless time, money and energy into maintaining a destructive status quo rather than muster their courage and take action. Egotism is a corporate cultural issue that someone in the business needs to own and tackle.

WHAT ENABLES EGOTISM TO THRIVE?

Egocentricity is clearly damaging to individuals and businesses and yet someone or something in the system enables it to thrive. Someone or something must gain by allowing egos to run rampage through corporate life.

There is something about the corporate culture that feeds hungry egos and keeps them firmly placed on their pedestals. Something about "the way we do things around here" that enables egos to sit comfortably right where they are for year upon year, generation upon generation. A history of sycophancy is an alarmingly common factor in the corporate world and might be a good place to start looking for clues. Think about the last board meeting or team briefing you went to. Who challenged the loudest contributor? Who dared to speak up to counter the ideas of the most articulate, manipulative colleague? Who had the courage to challenge the party line being pedalled by the CEO and his small protective circle of yes men? If no-one in this influential group has the tenacity to speak out against the egocentric leader, there is little chance that the culture of sycophancy will change.

PROTECTIVE LAYERS

A while ago I did some work with the board of a large multi-national business. The CEO had identified that individual board members, twenty-two of them, were not all facing in the same direction and working towards the same corporate goals. I began my work by having individual discussions with each board member. From those discussions it emerged that a key element of the problem was that the corporate goals were unclear and those that were clear were poorly communicated. By the CEO. But back in the boardroom none of these high powered, high profile men (they *were* all men) had the courage to stick his hand up and admit he didn't know what was going on. They were each afraid of being seen as weak or incompetent by their colleagues or, more importantly, by the CEO.

The CEO was an intriguing character. He came across as quietly charming, open to ideas, courteous, apparently keen to do well by his staff. He set a lot of store by loyalty. Many of these board members and indeed other employees, had been around for twenty years or more and were, in turn, fiercely loyal to him and to the business. He and his colleagues on the board had done much in recent years to take the company forward and create a global presence. But somehow they had got stuck. Their old ways of operating no longer worked for them. They were re-enacting a hierarchical pattern that had clearly served the company well in years gone by, but was now past its sell-by date. The CEO was desperate to get his board behind him and to be seen to be doing well by the shareholders.

Watching this man operate with the rest of his team was like watching someone working from inside a bubble. Just one of the board members was, metaphorically, allowed inside this bubble. But only as long as he agreed with the CEO, told him what he wanted to hear, or presented ideas that would broadly maintain the status quo and not cause too much disruption. This privileged individual was physically big, emotionally resilient, clear about his own agenda and fiercely protective of 'The Boss'. An effective henchman that no-one else on the board could hope to counter, move, or get round.

Communication between the CEO and the rest of his team as individuals was virtually non-existent. Some of them admitted privately that they wanted and needed an occasional hour with him about their careers, their hopes, their professional development, their ideas for the business. But somehow the discussion never happened. When they did find the courage to ask for time with him, the meeting would be scheduled in, then re-arranged, then somehow lost in the urgency of "more important" matters.

The boardroom became an egocentric playground. The CEO, whose own ego was fragile and in need of nurturing and protection by his yes-men, had become afraid to make a radical move or a courageous decision. Afraid to do anything that would incite criticism or represent risk. He had become stuck, frozen in time. Then there was the henchman who saw *himself* as the real power base in the company. He knew that anything he said or endorsed would be approved because to the CEO he represented safety. He had placed himself firmly at the centre of this particular universe and did everything to ensure he was going to stay there. He massaged the CEO's ego, told him what a wise and courageous man he was and ensured that all key decisions made about the way forward for the company kept the two of them secure in their respective positions.

The impact of their behaviour on the rest of the board was extraordinary and destructive. These two in their different ways had created a culture of fear and inactivity in which none of these able, intelligent men felt they could be creative or innovative. Many of them, in turn, were re-creating this culture within their own teams. There was a thread of fear running through the company that was almost tangible. There were bosses who had power and workers who didn't. At every level of the organisation. But it was inconceivable that these bosses would ever challenge upwards or risk having their own egos dented by inviting challenge from those who reported to them.

Layer upon layer of individuals afraid to make a good business decision without first asking "what's the impact on me?". Everyone kept in their place, no-one giving or getting honest feedback on their performance, no-one taking risks, no-one admitting to a mistake, so no chance of learning from it. A culture of fear, low self-esteem and no more than adequate productivity. That's what egos can do.

DOES BIGGEST MEAN BEST?

Think about your place of work. No doubt those at the most senior levels pride themselves on their big offices, their expensive cars, their carefully designed executive suites. There may even be a culture of inaccessibility wherein those with the real energy, drive and creativity have to wade through layers of bureaucracy, PAs and outer offices to be allowed an audience with the decision makers. Think about the titles those with power award themselves. Vice President. Executive Director. In the military and the police the titles are accompanied by gold braid and medals. In the clergy, fine robes and elevated, ornate headgear. In the judiciary, wigs and gowns. All protective layers designed to separate out the ordinary from the self-appointed extraordinary.

It's easy to argue that these symbols of grandiosity are just that. Symbols. Unimportant, trivial accoutrements that go with the job. But the powerful, if unspoken, message that's being sent is "I'm more important than you and I need some outward sign to let you and the rest of the world know it. I have more money, more power, higher status. If I want to I can get you to do exactly what I want because I'm in charge". So the ego muscles in and takes a stand, elbowing other lesser important beings out of the way. Pathetic and damaging. Moreover, potentially unnecessary. There are occasions, ceremonies, when it is entirely appropriate and respectful to don the uniform, polish the brass, climb into the limousine and initiate the formalities. But those occasions are few and far between and more often than not we simply hide behind the trappings and wrappings of success to mask who we really are and protect ourselves from our own insecurities.

AUTHENTIC LEADERSHIP: RUDOLPH GIULIANI

An authentic leader relies less on outward show and more on his inner sense of who he is, what he values and believes. He doesn't have to persuade or coerce people into following him by sending out these messages about his status. Rudolph Giuliani, mayor of New York at the time of the September 11 disaster, epitomises a leader who knows himself well, admits to his failings and treats those with whom he works with honour and respect. At a time when New York was in chaos and trauma he trod his way, literally and metaphorically, through the city with care, humility and a concern for others that went way beyond the call of duty. He displayed some of the skills we have come to label "soft"; he showed compassion and he listened. He allowed himself to feel pain and witness first hand the atrocity that unfolded before him. He scrambled alongside the fire-fighters and held the hands of the injured. He didn't have a uniform. Shortly after the planes hit he, like everyone else in the city, was in ragged, soot covered clothes that wouldn't have distinguished him from the next man. He couldn't make an important call on his cell-phone because no cell-phone would work. If he had had a big car to climb into it wouldn't have taken him anywhere because all the roads were blocked with debris from the twin towers. The point of this is not to glorify what he did, but to examine some of what lay behind his actions. Here is a man who, in the midst of a national disaster, managed to galvanise people into action, motivate them to behave with dignity and courage and make sense of chaos. He had none of the trappings of leadership at his disposal. Significantly Giuliani looked beyond himself. He concerned himself with what the *situation* needed, not what *he* needed. He wasn't being driven by a desire to appear virtuous or brave or superhuman. Here was a man working alongside people he respected, people he had spent time getting to know. The respect he received from his colleagues and the people of New York was a by-product of his actions, not something he set out to achieve as an end in itself. This wasn't about ego. This was authentic leadership.

EGOS PROVIDE ENERGY BUT AT WHAT COST?

Everyone has an ego. Everyone needs one as we will discover later in the book. The ego isn't inherently bad, but it *is* powerful. Particularly if its owner doesn't know how to handle it. A bit like a big powerful sports car, the ego in itself can't do any damage, but put it in the hands of an incompetent owner who doesn't understand it or recognise its potential and the opportunities for havoc and destruction are limitless.

Organisations have been living with the garrulous, demanding, hysterical, calculating behavioural manifestations of ego-driven individuals for decades. Some would say corporate life would be the poorer without the energy and charge that egos deliver. Boris Johnson, MP and editor of *The Spectator,* a political magazine with a taste for controversy, that itself exudes attitude and ego, has cultivated an opinionated, roguish persona which undoubtedly causes those closest to him to tear their hair out. But at the same time he brings an energy, a presence both to the political arena and to *The Spectator* that must generate excitement, enthusiasm and somehow just an expectation that things can be *different.* In 2004, Johnson became embroiled in a series of media scandals which depicted him as a philandering, heartless individual incapable of humility or compassion. Whether you support or loathe the man, the irony is that after an extraordinary few weeks in which his political and literary future were in doubt and *The Spectator's* reputation was looking vulnerable, circulation figures rose to an all-time high and many political commentators were endorsing Johnson as a future Tory leader.

Some might argue that we need leaders who dare to display outrageous self-belief, who are opinionated, forceful and driven by their own unshakeable agendas. Michael Maccoby writing for the *Harvard Business Review* suggests that, particularly during times of change, companies actually *need* leaders with what he describes as monumental egos. Narcissists, he says, believe they have the power to make things the way they want them. When the world needs shaping, Maccoby suggests, narcissists will stand ready with the mould.

If we look at organisations that thrive on the forces of their egos we might see:

- gloss and glamour
- a desire to be the best
- motivation
- drive
- enthusiasm
- a high profile

The ego-driven business and the people within it can be

- sexy
- sinful
- seductive

But there are costs. We know the ego brings with it energy, drive and compulsion, however problems arise when, like the incompetent owner of the powerful sports car, the individual is consistently driven by his ego rather than being aware of its existence and managing it appropriately; when resorting to ego-driven behaviour is his default position.

CHARISMATIC LEADERSHIP: AN ACCOMPLISHED PERFORMANCE?

When the ego is in charge, leadership is all about charisma, enigma and power play. With the ego in the driving seat leadership becomes merely an accomplished performance, with little substance or authenticity to underpin it. Ego-driven, charismatic leadership is seductive but fragile. Leaders who are both egotistical and unaware of their own personal drivers create businesses which, like them, lack any solid foundation.

Much of the work I do with individuals in organisations helps them bring into conscious awareness the needs and drives that impact heavily on their professional and personal lives. Needs and drives that rest in the subconscious which they can't initially identify and therefore work against them. If we *know* we are ego-driven we have choice. We can choose when and where to bring that ego into play. If we are very confident we can choose to admit to our egotism and acknowledge its strengths and weaknesses. Which in turn demonstrates a self-awareness and humility that gives others permission to be themselves, warts and all.

WHAT'S IN IT FOR ME?

We all do things for our own ends and we all run a personal agenda. The danger comes when we don't know it. The Reverend Robert Cotton, addressing a group of professionals in his local parish, said "I wouldn't trust a governor, a teacher or a priest who was in service solely for their own benefit. Neither would I trust a governor, a teacher or a priest who could not explain what was in it for them". There will always be people who are driven largely by an altruistic need to serve a wider cause and those at the other extreme who are in it for themselves. Most people are probably somewhere in the middle, but worryingly may not know or acknowledge where they sit on the line between the two extremes.

There has to be something more enduring than a needy ego shaping and maintaining the culture of the business or it will all implode. We have only to think of Nick Leeson and the Barings Bank debacle to see what can go wrong when big egos and weak leadership join forces. The BBC reported at the time: "the ego of a twenty-eight year old trader on the Singapore Monetary Exchange and the greed and stupidity of a two hundred and thirty three year-old bank had combined to destroy an investment empire and in the process stunned the world". The key players in this drama were so busy worrying about their image and reputation that they failed to notice or acknowledge the millions of dollars Leeson was siphoning off into "error account 88888" to cover his monumental trading losses. Leeson's ego was so fragile that he was driven to continue on his path of self and corporate destruction for fear of losing his status and the trappings that went with his ego-fed career. Yes, sometimes we do need big egos to drive us forward, to create energy and enthusiasm, but the danger comes when those in charge look *only* for external approval and seek *purely* external references for who they are and what they do, rather than making their decisions from a solid base of self-worth. At best they will become stressed and at worst generate corporate instability.

THE GOOD, THE BAD AND THE UGLY

The ego is destructive, energising, seductive, manipulating and motivating. We might be aware of the power of our own ego or the egos that play out in our places of work, or we might not. Whether we are in big business, the public sector, the armed forces, the emergency services, the clergy or self-employment, lack of awareness isn't good enough. It's too costly an option.

2

THE EGO: WHAT IT IS AND WHAT IT DOES

WHO NEEDS AN EGO?

We all do. Egos have energy. They drive us forward. They motivate us. As we shall see later on in this chapter, they help us meet our most basic, primal needs for power, status and recognition. The ego is all about "me". Literally translated from Latin, the word ego means "I".

In common parlance, the words ego and egotism have become emotive and value-laden. They are words that have come to describe elements of the human psyche that are bad – something to be hidden away or denied.

NARCISSISM

We talk about big egos, inflated egos and fragile egos. Often we have no real understanding of the ego's drives or origins. When we talk about ego-driven behaviour we usually mean behaviour that is somehow destructive or unhelpful. The word "egotism" conjures up thoughts of over-bearing, self-centred individuals who are impervious to the needs and sensibilities of others and whose only question is "what's in it for me?". What we're usually talking about is the narcissistic element of egotism, the part of us that wants to know:

- how will I look?
- what will people think of me?
- what do I stand to gain?
- what might I lose?
- how do I maintain control?

If you are primarily ego-driven you are at the centre of your own universe. Narcissism is a big part of your psyche. In Greek mythology Narcissus was a youth who pined away for the love of his own image. Narcissistic leaders revel in their own image and gain almost sensual gratification from praise and adulation. Of course as part of normal development we all go through a stage of self-absorption and obsessive mirror-gazing, but most of us grow out of it and get real. For some though, the narcissistic drives get so firmly lodged in our psyches that they are never set aside or allowed to develop into a healthy, adult self-respect. As an egotistical leader there will be a large part of you, the narcissistic part, that is never satisfied, never good enough, always needy, always craving that big fat elusive cherry that sits on top of someone else's cake.

But what lies beneath this behaviour? What's the ego really about? What's going on in our heads, in our guts, in our hearts? If narcissism isn't the whole story, what else is there to know?

EGO-LESS OR EGO FREE?

We don't have a word or phrase in common usage that implies any positive manifestation of the ego. If we were to play around with possibilities we might come up with "ego-less", but that's not possible. And I would question the desirability of an ego-less individual or organisation. We all have egos and we all need them. They serve us well in protecting us from the unfettered cravings of what Freud described as the Id: the primal, child-like force within us that strives to get our needs met regardless of the costs or implications to ourselves or others. The ego helps to protect us from anxiety and motivates us to move forward. Ego energy can be dynamic, thrusting and focused. Perhaps we could talk about the "healthy ego", the "balanced ego", or even the "nourished ego".

Although we can't be ego-less we can be ego free. Ego-free leaders, ego-free organisations and cultures *recognise and accept* their ego needs. They don't try to deny them or hide them away. Neither are they blindly driven by them. Ego-free leaders, organisations and cultures acknowledge their egos, but don't expend excessive amounts of time and energy massaging them. They are free from the tyranny of the ego. Later on in the book we will take a closer look at ego-free individuals and cultures. We will examine how to deal with them, how to create and nurture them and what to do if you find yourself working in an ego-driven organisation, or with an ego-driven colleague.

FREUD

Where does the concept of the ego originate? In order to get a better, deeper grasp of what we're dealing with here let's take a step back and examine where the idea of the ego originated and what it means for each of us as individuals.

The psychoanalyst Sigmund Freud became well known for his research into how the personality is "organised" and how our conscious and subconscious thought processes influence our behaviour. Freud divided the personality into three structures; the id, the ego and the superego. Whilst these are not physical structures – if you sliced open a brain you wouldn't see separate physical areas – they are notionally three separate, but interrelated, parts of the mind that influence who we are and what we do.

The id

Let's start with the id. The word "id" comes from the Latin word "it" and is the part of our personality that develops when we are infants. The id operates entirely out of the unconscious – that is, we have no awareness of its drives, its urges, or its influences over us. The id is closely linked to our biological needs, it's main aim being to get food, air, water, sex, or whatever else we need for basic survival. The id grasps and clutches at what it needs without paying any heed to the wants and need of others. It doesn't care about approval, rules, social norms or niceties. It wants what it wants and it wants it now. It has no concept of delayed gratification. It doesn't recognise fear or sense danger; its sole purpose is to reduce the tension built up through hunger, thirst, sexual frustration or whatever else our bodies may crave. Freud describes this drive towards immediate gratification as the pleasure principle. While we can't "see" any of these drives we become all too aware of the outward manifestations of the id – what filters through to the surface and becomes our behaviour. What we often notice in others (and maybe even ourselves) is behaviour that is impulsive, irrational, narcissistic, exaggeratedly self-loving and self-centred, actions that are geared towards self-preservation. Id-driven behaviour can appear illogical, irrational, often with little ability to inhibit impulses or to discriminate between the real and the unreal. Its own needs are paramount and it pays no heed to the existence of an external world. This, then, is where the ego comes in.

The ego

The ego (the Latin word for "I") is the decision-making component of the personality. Like the id it is also deeply concerned with self-preservation, but whereas the id's raw energy wants gratification at any cost, the ego metaphorically takes a step back and says "OK, this is what we need, but lets consider the implications before we take it. Let's look at the options, let's wait a while and think about the rules we are transgressing, the practical implications of our actions". So the ego in a sense becomes the mediator between the primitive urges of the Id and the environment, or context, in which it finds itself. In contrast to the id's pleasure-seeking nature, the ego obeys what Freud describes as the reality principle. Although it gets energy from the id to take action, the ego concerns itself with ensuring the safety and self-preservation of the individual. It has the capacity to distinguish between reality and fantasy, tolerate moderate amounts of tension and engage in rational thought processes to satisfy instinctual needs appropriately without endangering self or others. The ego then is the seat of intellectual processes and problem solving.

The superego

The superego is sometimes described as the moral-ethical arm of the personality. The Latin translation of the word is "over-I". Whereas the id wants gratification now and the ego concerns itself with getting needs met safely and appropriately, the superego's role is to ensure that we function effectively in society. The superego aims to develop a set of values, norms and ethics that are reasonably compatible with the social group the individual finds himself in. Freud's theory suggests that whereas we are born with the id and the ego, we don't develop a superego until we are between three and five years old, when we start to take notice of the messages coming from our parents and teachers about what's right and wrong, good and bad, moral and immoral. To begin with we internalise or believe only what these significant figures tell us about good and bad behaviour. We put every effort into living up to the parental ideal, until our world broadens (through school, religion, peer groups) and we begin to absorb and incorporate the rules and norms of a wider group, beyond our family. As we grow we develop a *conscience*. We subconsciously develop a capacity for guilt, punitive self-evaluation and moral prohibitions when we feel we are not living up to the standards our parents or peer groups set. The "shoulds" and "oughts" start to creep in and influence our decisions, without our being aware of them. Because we are not aware of them, we cannot hold them up to the light and scrutinise them for their relevance and validity in our current context.

Conscience vs excellence

While one aspect of the superego is to provide us with a conscience, its other role is to drive us towards the pursuit of excellence. A pursuit that is derived from whatever our parents or carers approved and valued. The individual seeks to achieve standards of excellence which in turn leads to a sense of self-esteem and pride. Freud described this drive as the *ego ideal*.

The locked cupboard

What we often see played out in the corporate arena, particularly with women high fliers, is a tension between the inhibiting pull of the *conscience* that pulls us back and the rewarding aspect of the *ego ideal* that strives to push us forward. I was recently working with an extremely capable woman, a finance director who displayed intellectual ability, pragmatism and insight. During the course of the coaching sessions it became clear that she was frustrated with her current role. We gradually discovered that she was ambitious, but surprisingly to both of us, she appeared to lack the confidence to try for a bigger role. After spending some time exploring the belief system that underpinned her caution we found lurking a whole set of parental messages. Messages that had been metaphorically stored away in a locked cupboard at the back of her mind. On the one hand she was storing messages of support for her intellectual ability, but on the other, there were a set of equally clear injunctions that broadly made it clear that nice girls didn't show off or place themselves in the limelight. So conflicting messages from her conscience and her ego ideal had been keeping her stuck, unable to move forward professionally. Through coaching this able woman was able to unlock the cupboard, take out the contents and examine them. By bringing some of these stored messages into her conscious awareness she was able to evaluate them critically and make a well reasoned decision about her career path. A decision that was now based on current information rather than historical data. She has now successfully made the transition into a bigger role.

Ego Defence Mechanisms: the bit we see

It sounds at this point as though what we normally describe as ego-driven behaviour is, in Freudian terms, id-driven behaviour. The "I want it and I want it now and damn you" approach to life. But let's take the Freudian theme a stage further. In order to keep a lid on the wayward, irrepressible id, the ego develops various strategies, or defence mechanisms, to keep the id contained and to protect us from overwhelming anxiety. When the id starts playing up the ego reacts in one of two ways. It either *blocks out* the demand the id is making or *distorts* it to such a degree that its intensity is reduced or deflected. So, when the id's demands become too difficult, too much to bear, the ego steps in and takes action.

Defence mechanisms share two common characteristics. Firstly they operate at an unconscious level and are therefore self-deceptive. Secondly, in order to reduce our anxiety, they distort, deny, or falsify our perception of reality. Let's take a look at the key defence mechanisms that work away in the depths of our subconscious, dictating our behaviour and impacting on our relationships with ourselves and others.

Repression   If you work for the emergency services you're probably facing human tragedy almost daily. At first you react. You are shocked by the awful events that unfold before you. You have flash-backs to the horrendous things you have witnessed. You don't sleep. But gradually, you seem to become immune. You start sleeping properly again. It becomes easier to trip back into your default position. You laugh and joke. Black humour takes the place of distress.

Freud describes repression as the main ego defence because it is the most adept mechanism we use to protect us from anxiety. Sometimes described as *motivated forgetting*, repression is a process of wiping out distressing thoughts and feelings from our consciousness. The word *denial* is probably one we are more familiar with. We deny or erase emotionally traumatic past events. The firefighter who was unable to save the small child and sees this inability as a significant personal failure might eventually be quite unable to recall or describe the event. The diligent, caring teacher who didn't spot the warning signs when the bright pupil failed her exams erases the whole distressing episode from her memory.

Although repression can be useful in that it can save us from the symptoms of anxiety, the relief it provides is not without cost. Repressed thoughts don't just disappear. They remain active in the subconscious and if we're going to keep them at bay we will use significant and continuous emotional energy to do so. This persistent drain on our resources will eventually have a serious detrimental impact on the energy we have for our work and play. And it's quite likely that we won't be able to keep a lid on these repressed memories for ever. They will leak out harmlessly as dreams, "Freudian slips", jokes, or more destructively, as psychosomatic ailments such as ulcers, impotence and frigidity.

Projection A nifty little devil, this one. Some leaders might argue that projection, of all the defence mechanisms, is the one they would keep if they had to jettison all the others from the boat in order to survive... you know the routine. Projection helps you, the *occasionally* fallible leader blame other people for your own shortcomings. How useful is that? If you fail to get a report out on time it's not *your* fault. It's all those other idiots who didn't get the information to you when you needed it. It's the inadequate briefing you had in the first place, or the administrative system, or... Projection enables you to attribute all your unacceptable thoughts, feelings and behaviours onto other people or the environment. You become adept at blaming someone or something else for your own shortcomings.

Taken to the extreme, projection enables us to attribute all the parts of ourselves we don't like onto other "types" or other groups of people. We turn individuals, groups and ultimately nations, into scapegoats, as we attribute our own negative personal characteristics onto convenient receptors, be they the archetypal villain, or the ethnic or racial stereotype. The Nazis effectively disowned their own unpalatable traits and offloaded them onto the Jews. In Freudian terms they rendered a whole ethnic group worthless and reprehensible. What the Nazis failed to acknowledge was that it was their own reprehensible behaviour and their own worthlessness they couldn't own up to, so they "dumped" these qualities on another race.

Think about the sub-cultures that develop in our places of work. Groups of people become notorious within the organisation for being aggressively competitive, for being malicious, for being soft, for being laissez-faire. Of course there may be some justification for these groups of people attracting these labels. A tutor of mine once said "we don't project onto a blank screen". Within the subculture that has emerged there may be, or there may once have been, an incident, or a person with a particular trait, who caused this group to attract the label it has. But at a subconscious level, what has happened is that this group has unwittingly become a vessel that others fill with all the bits of themselves they don't like. By dumping my aggressive competitiveness onto another group or individual I can forget about it. It's not mine. I don't need to let it trouble me. The messages I received from my parents about being fair and reasonable can stay intact and I can quietly and smugly reassure myself that I am still the good girl and it's that other lot who are bad.

Displacement We're big, we're important and we're clever. And we've had a bad day. The Big Boss has been undermining, sarcastic and has trashed the work we've so laboriously produced. What do we do? Take an assertive stand? Tell her reasonably and calmly how we feel and let her know the impact her behaviour has on our productivity? Like hell we do. We shout at the very nice lady who serves the sandwiches because she doesn't have any ham and mustard left. What we're probably not aware of at the time is that the nice lady with no ham and mustard is simply a substitute target. The original object of our hostility, our boss, has been replaced by someone who is far less threatening and has far less power to take retaliatory action. And it's not always *another* person that becomes that substitute. We're just as likely to turn our hostility onto *ourselves*. We become impatient and angry with our own perceived shortcomings, which, if taken to extreme, can bring about feelings of self-deprecation and ultimately lead to depression.

Rationalisation   When it comes to coping with frustration and anxiety the ego is a key player. When our self-esteem and reputation are in jeopardy the ego steps in to distort reality and make the picture fit the frame. Rationalisation means false reasoning. The ego takes a piece of irrational behaviour and tries to make it appear rational and therefore justifiable to oneself and others. Imagine it. You are in a powerful leadership role and you've ballsed up big time. You've displayed poor judgement and you're staring the dreaded "f" word – failure – in the face. But don't worry. Your errors of judgement, your misdemeanours and foibles can be explained away in an instant – through the magic of rationalisation. We've all heard of the "sour grapes" described in Aesop's fable. A fox couldn't reach the grapes he wanted so decided they were probably sour anyway and that really he didn't want them. We get passed over for promotion and decide that we didn't really want the job anyway. It would have had too much of an impact on our family and social life and we could never in a million years work with the guy that would have been our new boss. And anyway it's probably time to move on and look for a role in an organisation that's not run by fools and will recognise our genius... In our minds we are "making sense" of an unpalatable situation. Useful, maybe in the short term, but in the long term, the energy we put into quelling our real emotional responses erodes our health, our sanity and our authenticity.

Regression Can you think of a leader who has tantrums? Pouts? Shouts or gives people the silent treatment? Does this leader flip into a coy, manipulative, "poor little me" routine when threatened? Or perhaps, when they're cornered, they take ridiculous risks, rebel against authority or become destructive and critical. What you're probably experiencing is regression. A reversion to the child-like behaviour that got them out of trouble when they were young. They're locked into a pattern of responding to danger that may no longer be appropriate, but, because it's happening out of awareness, they are powerless to change. Dangerous. Not authentic.

TRAITS OF THE EGO-DRIVEN INDIVIDUAL

So how can you tell that the Freudian forces are at work? The ego-driven individual may display some or all of the following traits:

- obvious self-focus in interpersonal exchanges: it's all about me
- lack of empathy – cannot view the world from another's perspective
- hypersensitivity to slights or perceived insults
- favours people who admire and affirm him
- constant need for attention
- pretends to be more important than he is
- boasts and exaggerates his achievements and talents
- claims to be an expert
- expects to be recognised as superior
- believes he is special and can only be understood by, or associate with, other special people (will claim to have the best lawyer, consultant etc in the field)
- has a sense of entitlement and unreasonable expectations of favourable treatment and compliance with his expectations (why should he wait in the queue?)
- is exploitative: takes advantage of others to achieve his own ends
- believes others envy him
- dominates the space
- demands perfection and immediate gratification
- sacrifices people indiscriminately
- resists change that threatens to undermine his position
- intimidates and manipulates others

Who would have thought it? We casually bandy the term ego around without ever realising quite what we mean by it or knowing exactly what's behind the ego-driven behaviour we find so difficult. The ego clearly has its uses. As a quick fix, a short-term solution, the ego can kick in and provide us with immediate relief and gratification. A bit of blame here, a touch of denial there, mixed with a liberal seasoning of regression and rationalisation can ease our way through a difficult day in the office and leave us feeling that we are in charge, coping, keeping on top. But what of the longer term impact of relying heavily on the ego, never seeking to question or uncover its motivations? What harm do we do ourselves, our colleagues and our organisations if we never find the courage to take a critical look at what we're doing and why?

Egotists come in many guises and may have a place in corporate life. They can be charismatic, visionary and inspirational. They can appear confident and clear with big personalities; charmers who can convert the masses with their rhetoric. Old-paradigm leadership theory would argue that egotistical leaders are good for business, especially during times of transition when what's needed is clarity and drive. Gifted strategists and courageous risk takers, they drive their companies to greatness. But they also have a dark side that can obliterate their careers – and their companies.

3

WHY LEADERS DON'T NEED BIG ONES

THE WORLD OF THE CELEBRITY CHEF

Jamie Oliver is a celebrity chef who has risen to fame and fortune in recent years. He has inspired and informed television viewers with his understated leadership style and his unique approach to achieving excellence and perfection with and through those that work with him.

Jamie Oliver is a confident yet self-effacing man who achieves great things by knowing his own principles and values and articulating them quietly and repeatedly until someone listens. Without shouting, without ranting, without personal criticism of those around him, Jamie Oliver has commanded the attention of the Prime Minister and the UK education system in his quest to put children's nutrition on the government's agenda. He is a working-class lad with a passion. And he communicates that passion in a way that says "I know I am right but I don't have to take away *your* dignity to prove it". He knows who he is. He knows what he stands for.

A couple of years ago Jamie Oliver opened a new restaurant "Fifteen". Nothing remarkable about that. Except that the young men and women Oliver recruited to work there were young and unemployed – some would say unemployable – with no experience of cooking or the restaurant business. No-one would finance the deal – it was too big a risk, so Oliver, we are told, financed it himself. He had an insurmountable belief that he could turn these young people into chefs and entrepreneurs. And he did. The whole journey was televised. Success and failure were publicly documented. What you sensed from day one was that this was a man with bucket loads of self-awareness and self-esteem. This was ego-free leadership personified. You had a sense that you were watching the *real* man in action. This wasn't an act for the cameras. The confidence he had in his own judgement and ability translated into a confidence to work alongside those young people without resorting to power play. When the press trashed him you saw him having a quiet sob. It was his emotional liberation and frankness that won him acclaim as an individual and as a leader. Money, power, a social conscience and emotional awareness. How cool is that? Egotistical leaders eat your heart out.

Jamie Oliver *allows* people to see his greatness. His ego is strong enough not to have to force his greatness upon them. If they don't notice it, so be it. He knows it's there.

HIGH-PROFILE COLLEAGUES

Contrast Oliver's approach with that of some of his high-profile colleagues. The celebrity chefs who also have a passion for their trade, but who like drama, who throw their weight about demanding deference and eliciting fear in those that trail in their wake. They shout. They swear. They hurl pans across kitchens. These guys don't cry. They belittle and undermine their team members, reducing *them* to tears, never revealing their own vulnerability. If something goes wrong it's other fools who are to blame. It's *their* incompetence and sheer stupidity that are causing problems for the great men in charge. But if something goes exceptionally well… then we know who will take the credit. These men are addicted to blame and adulation in equal measure.

These high-profile chefs achieve great things, but at what cost? Certainly there's a personal cost to those who work with them. Confident capable people are reduced to inarticulation and self-doubt in the wake of their tyranny. In order for these men to be right others need to be wrong. They have to win. Through their behaviour, these chefs *force* people to see their greatness. Their egos are too fragile to leave it to chance. And if others don't notice their greatness they have little left because deep down they're not at all sure they're so great.

SELF-AWARENESS AND AUTHENTICITY

Oliver and his celebrity colleagues all have egos. Every leader has an ego. That in itself isn't the problem. There's only a problem if that ego-driven leader isn't *aware* of the extent and nature of his ego-drives. If he's not *aware*, he's not in charge of himself, his behaviour, or his thought processes. An unaware leader is a leader out of control, careering along a road with no firm grip on the wheel. He will thrash around, lurching from one drama to the next, leaving a trail of misery and destruction in his wake. His behaviour will become manipulative and harmful to himself and those around him as he gets locked into destructive patterns of blame, projection, denial and rationalisation. The unaware leader becomes so absorbed with, and driven by, his own needs and insecurities that he eventually becomes disconnected from the world around him. He loses – or never finds – the ability to have any meaningful, authentic dialogue with his colleagues and business partners. He becomes isolated and self-protected, with a distorted sense of reality.

EGO-FREE LEADERSHIP IS NO LONGER OPTIONAL

The imperative economic need to rid our organisations of ego-driven leadership is both significant and urgent. The ego-driven leader whose behaviour is needy, manipulative and lacking authenticity will not be able to adapt to a rapidly changing, fiercely competitive global economy. The ego-driven leader who lacks self-awareness and self-respect will form toxic relationships and ultimately create toxic organisations which are so self-obsessed and neurotic that they lack the capacity to take a realistic view of the threats and opportunities that surround them. The ego-driven leader has an impaired capacity to think clearly, to learn, to choose and make appropriate decisions in the face of turbulence and change. His reserves of self-esteem and self-awareness are so low that he cannot possibly function at his full capacity. His impairment will filter out and contaminate every level of the organisation.

THE DARK SIDE OF THE UNAWARE EGO-DRIVEN LEADER

A bleak and over-dramatic picture? Think about some of the ego-driven leaders you know and see how they measure up against the following list of typical traits. Then think about the impact of these traits on the leader's own effectiveness, on the people around them and ultimately to the bottom line and what the company is setting out to achieve. Suddenly our tolerance of egotistical leadership begins to look rather foolish, inappropriate, costly...

Invincibility

Egotistical leaders hanker after adulation and success and eventually begin to feel invincible. They ignore cautionary words and take flagrant risks. They listen only to information they seek and will want to dominate those around them

Sensitivity to criticism

Egotists are unimaginably thin-skinned and can't tolerate dissent. They *say* they want teamwork but really want yes-men. As more independent minded players get pushed out succession becomes a problem

Lack of empathy

They crave empathy but are not empathic themselves. They can be brutally exploitative. They may see a need for *others* to develop touchy-feely skills but it's not for them. They struggle with intimacy

Intense desire to compete

They are relentless and ruthless in their pursuit of victory, often unrestrained by conscience and convinced that threats abound. Organisations led by egotists are generally characterised by intense internal competition. Their passion to win is marked by both the promise of glory and the primitive danger of extinction. Andy Grove of Intel once said "only the paranoid survive".

NOTE: The table on pages 57–9 is adapted from *Narcissistic Leaders: The Incredible Pros, the Inevitable Cons* by Michael Maccoby in *Harvard Business Review*, January 2000.

Lack of self-knowledge and restraining anchors

Egotists can become unrealistic dreamers. They might nurture grand schemes and harbour the illusion that only circumstances or enemies block their success.

Inability to embrace change

Change is seen as a threat that could undermine their power, status and position in the system. When under pressure to bring about change they may stonewall by asking for excessive and unnecessarily detailed reports, block access to funding and resources or indulge in character assassination and spreading misinformation.

A tendency towards grandiosity

They over-estimate their own abilities. They come to believe they are invincible and all-powerful. Nothing and no-one can get in their way. They promote the idea that you can go round them but not through them.

Paranoia

They are self-protective and wary, constantly on the look out for the enemy.

Addiction to adulation

Ego-driven leaders are hooked on praise and adoration. They have a constant and often petulant need to be told of their greatness.

Selective listening

They filter out any information that doesn't fit with their idea of reality. They listen only to the messages they want to hear.

Inability to learn from others

Egotists like making speeches, telling, transmitting and indoctrinating, but are less open to hearing others' views and suggestions. They will dominate meetings and allow little opportunity for debate.

Distaste for personal development

They don't want to change and as long as they are successful, they don't think they have to. They will resist any form of coaching or mentoring for themselves and when they mentor others they will often lack the ability to support and nurture another's development. If they do, grudgingly, agree to a mentoring role they will only maintain an interest if their protégée shows signs of becoming pale reflections of themselves.

Inadequate decision making

Day-to-day decisions are based primarily on personal preferences, hidden agendas and the tyranny of office politics. Business benefits become less important than image.

CAN YOU AFFORD IT?

If you run a business can you afford to continue to collude with this behaviour? Can you afford to go on recruiting leaders with the same destructive characteristics? What do you do if you recognise *yourself* in this description? How do you manage your own egotistical traits? How do you manage the egotistical leaders that run rife in your business? Before answering those and other ego-related questions lets take a look at another kind of leader. The ego-free leader who is self-aware and has a high level of self-esteem. The leader whose ego is more balanced, better managed. Let's see why size really does matter.

THE EGO-FREE LEADER

Ego-free leadership is built on two fundamental factors: self-esteem and self-awareness. These two building blocks will underpin everything the ego-free leader does and the extent of his self-esteem and self-awareness will have a direct bearing on his personal success, his authenticity, the quality of his working relationships and ultimately on the success of the business.

The ego-free leader is willing to look at not just his behaviour, but his beliefs, values and emotional needs. He is not ego-less but he is ego free. Because he knows himself well he knows when his ego is stepping in and playing up. He can exercise a degree of choice over whether he lets it take over. He is free from the tyranny of his ego. He is free to make choices. This leader is, and will inspire others to be, strong, resilient and ultimately more productive both personally and professionally. The leader with high levels of self-esteem and self-awareness is powerful. This isn't about power *over* others. It's about power *with* others. The truly powerful leader doesn't need others to be wrong in order that he might be right. He doesn't need to command and control in every situation. He inspires and leads with humility and grace.

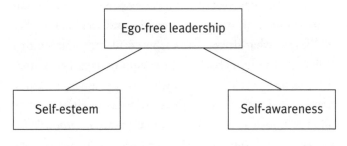

Self-esteem

If we have high self-esteem we feel competent to cope with the basic challenges of life. We believe we deserve happiness and fulfilment and we generally experience the world as an open, honest place that will treat us fairly and isn't out to get us. We are realistic about the threats we face but we don't display undue paranoia in the face of day-to-day challenges. If we have high self-esteem we cope better with adversity than those with low self-esteem. Some of the most successful entrepreneurs are those with one or more bankruptcies behind them, but who have had the courage and confidence to pick themselves up and start again. If we have high self-esteem we will treat ourselves with respect. And because we treat ourselves in that way we will treat others with respect, goodwill and fairness. We don't expect rejection, humiliation, treachery or betrayal at every turn. Our behaviour and expectations become a self-fulfilling prophecy. People respond to trust and openness *with* trust and openness. We receive what we expect. Self-esteem is the reputation we get with ourselves.

Self-awareness

If we have a high level of self-awareness we will have a fair understanding of our own strengths and weaknesses. We will know what drives us, be able to identify the limiting beliefs that hold us back and the empowering beliefs that drive us forward. We will be aware of our values and know how they sit with the values of the organisations we inhabit. Above all we will know that we are *responsible* for our own lives, our own happiness, our own success. We will recognise that blame, criticism, denial, rationalisation and tantrums might give us a quick satisfaction fix, but ultimately they make a poor strategy for success.

If we are self-aware we know that *we* are responsible for:

- the achievement of our own desires
- our choices and actions
- the level of consciousness we bring to our work
- the level of consciousness we bring to our relationships
- our behaviour with our colleagues, associates and clients
- the way we spend our time
- the quality of our communication
- our personal happiness
- the values we live by
- our own personal development and maintenance of our self-esteem

It's easy to see why ego-driven leaders are motivated to stay the way they are. Personal development takes energy, courage, determination and clarity of vision. Self-awareness and self-development are often lumped into the "soft" category. The stuff you do when you're going through your mid-life crisis. It's not for the macho leadership types who put on a brave face, keep a stiff upper lip and get on with the job. Because the macho types who hide behind an inauthentic mask don't have the personal resources, the confidence or the strength to take a look at themselves and ask the fundamental question: "who am I?". High-flying executives spend a fortune on training programmes that promise to give them impact and gravitas. For those who know themselves well, who live their lives by a congruent set of values, who have robust self-esteem and a high level of self-awareness, these programmes do deliver. They offer them a way of behaving which reflects who they really are. But for those who don't know who they are or what they stand for trying to "train in" impact and gravitas is like putting a sticking plaster on a broken arm. It won't hold up. It will fall apart. People will see it for what it is: a futile attempt to shore up something that's broken with a superficial prop. If you *do* know who you are the behaviour bit's easy. If you *don't* know who you are any behaviour will do. People will see through it anyway.

HOW TO RECOGNISE AN EGO-FREE LEADER

Flexibility

Ego-free leadership transcends leadership style. An ego-free leader can be collaborative, authoritative, inclusive, commanding and nurturing. She doesn't blindly adhere to one leadership style because that's the only one that keeps her ego intact, keeps her looking good, keeps her in control, keeps her on her pedestal. She can afford to let go, experiment, occasionally get it wrong.

Adaptability

Openness to change. The ego-free leader doesn't fear change or see it as a threat to his power and position.

Altruism

The ego-free leader is altruistic but not blindly so. He will want to know "what's in it for me" but that won't be his only question. He will be equally concerned with what's in it for the business, the team, the brand identity. The ego-free leader acknowledges his own self-interest, will talk about it and will encourage others to do the same

Humility

Ego-free leaders are respected not because they demand respect but because they command it. They don't shout, flout or parade their successes. They allow others to *discover* their wisdom. They let those around them *experience* their value and their worth.

Empathy

Ego-free leaders aren't needy in the same way that ego-driven leaders are. Because they're not forever having to shore themselves up emotionally they can afford to let go and walk in another man's shoes, get an understanding of what someone else is feeling or experiencing without risking the loss of their own identity or status.

Power

The power of the ego-free leader is deeply embedded, long lasting and resilient. The ego-free leader has power *with* others not power *over* them. He can allow others to be as powerful as he is. He is assertive not aggressive. He is comfortable with winning and he is comfortable when others win. For him to be right he doesn't need to make others wrong.

Makes sound decisions based on facts not image

The ego-free leader will want to make the best decision for all concerned – even if that decision doesn't leave her in the best possible light. She knows when to step forward and make a decision and when to step back and let others make it. She can hear others' opinions and give them appropriate consideration without fear of losing face.

Inspires others to be confident

The ego-free leader invites authentic dialogue and robust criticism. He creates opportunities for challenge and debate. He encourages the timid to be audacious and those who lack self-confidence to celebrate their own successes.

THE LEADERSHIP LEGACY

What of the legacy of the celebrity chefs we examined earlier? Perhaps one of the greatest tests of a leader is what he or she leaves behind him. Jamie Oliver is setting out to make a real and lasting difference, not just to the fifteen young people he sponsored in the Fifteen venture, but more widely in raising public awareness of the value of good quality nutrition. No doubt all of these high-profile chefs are, in their own way, setting out to make a real difference in their own professional spheres. But how many of them want that difference to endure when they have moved on? Or must the glory move on with them?

THE EGO-FREE LEADER LEAVES GLORY BEHIND

The ego-free leader does not need to take glory with him when he moves on. His self-esteem and self-awareness are such that he can create something great but he doesn't have to be attached to it. It doesn't have to be part of him.

CORPORATE IMPLICATIONS

Leaders often fail to recognise that "who they are" affects virtually every aspect of the organisation. Many do not appreciate the extent of their power as role models. Their smallest behaviours are noted and absorbed by those around them, not necessarily consciously and reflected via those they influence throughout the organisation. A leader who has integrity, who treats others with respect, gives an

Table 3.1: Two different legacies

The ego-free leader's legacy is to:	The ego-driven leader's legacy is to:
• **Be dispensable** He acknowledges that his greatest successes are with, and through others. He empowers them to do well long after he is gone.	• **Create excellence that moves on with him** His main interest is his own reputation. The lasting success of the business is only of interest if it makes him look good.
• **Select superb successors** The ego-free leader recruits people who are as good as, if not better than him. He selects people who are good for the on-going success of the business, not people who will reinforce his image.	• **Select successors who are barely as good as him** His ego isn't strong enough to risk being out-shone.
• **Create an environment in which his successors can shine more brightly than him** His interest and energy go into generating organisational excellence rather than personal glory.	• **Create an environment in which he has power over others** He must always be top-dog. His self-esteem rests on being more powerful and prominent than those around him. He must always be right and always be the best.

unspoken message that this is the standard that has been set. This is the culture. This is the way we do things around here. A leader who is out of touch with himself and his colleagues in any real sense will become a microcosm of the wider organisation. If the person at the centre of the organisation lacks awareness and authenticity the layers of people around him will also lack awareness and authenticity. Slice through an onion and you will see each layer looks the same. Unless we have the courage to take an honest look at ourselves, honour and keep what's useful and respectfully let go of what isn't, we can never hope to be authentic leaders, colleagues or employees.

TAKE A LOOK AT YOURSELF

So what do you do if you suspect you are an egotistical leader, but haven't yet "come out"? Do you carry on hiding? Do you carry on being a mystery to yourself? Do you continue pretending that your strategies are working for you and that you are getting the best from your colleagues and staff? Do you stoically and defensively assure yourself that you are getting optimum results for the business? Or do you find the courage to unlock the cupboard and take a cold hard look at the contents? The higher the self-esteem and self-awareness of the leader, that is, the more ego-free he or she is, the more likely it is that he or she can inspire others. A mind that does not trust itself cannot evoke the best in the minds of others. Nor can leaders inspire the best in others if their primary need, arising from their insecurity, is to prove themselves right and others wrong.

If you want to know whether you are an egotistical or an ego-free leader take a look at the following statements that describe some of the typical traits of the ego-free leader.

Take time to think about each one. On a scale of one to ten, ten being closest to the statement, give yourself a score. For each response you give, think of examples, things you have said and done, that reinforce that response. Write your answers down and, if you have the courage, show both questions and answers to someone you know and trust and ask them for feedback on the authenticity of your self-appraisal. If you can muster even more courage use the Egotistical Leadership Peer Assessment in Chapter 5 to see what others think of you.

Ego-free leadership statement	Self score (1–10)
I can ask myself "who am I?" and know the answer	
I work on my own self-esteem and self-awareness: I take time out to explore and discuss my beliefs, my values, my doubts and my personal strategies for dealing with those around me	
I am confident in my own personal integrity. I keep my promises and honour my commitments. I treat peers, employees and contacts outside the business with honesty, fairness and dignity.	
I acknowledge my own needs – e.g. for praise, harmony, status, victory – but I am informed, not driven by them. I accept those needs as part of who I am but I don't let them contaminate my interactions with others.	
I know the difference between a real threat and something that fuels my paranoia.	

Ego-free leadership statement	Self score (1–10)
I invite feedback on who I am and what I do. And I accept it with grace and gratitude, whether or not it fits with my ideal picture.	
I learn from others, no matter what their status within the company.	
I listen more than I speak.	
The success of the business is important to me. And I'm honest with myself about what's in it for me.	
When people have spoken to me they know they have been heard: when I listen to people I clear my mind of internal and external clutter: prejudice, agendas, more urgent tasks...	
No matter who I am speaking to my behaviour is respectful, free from condescension, sarcasm and blame.	
I treat people well because I believe that's what they deserve. It's not just something I've learnt on a leadership programme.	
If I treat someone badly I put my dignity to one side and apologise.	
I am confident enough to show empathy. I let people know that I have an understanding of their feelings and intentions as well as their statements.	
People around me know they are seen and heard, without judgement blame or prejudice.	
I set clear, fair standards for behaviour and performance and support people in achieving them.	

Ego-free leadership statement	Self score (1–10)
I don't hand down orders from on high. I give reasons and explanations when appropriate.	
People can say "I don't know" or "I'll find out" without fear of ridicule or retribution.	
I can say "I don't know" or "I'll find out" without feeling weak or out of control.	
People can make mistakes and I will explore with them what went wrong and how they can do things better next time, without blame, sarcasm or undermining. I want them to learn and keep their self-esteem intact.	
I manage disputes by focusing on the task and the facts, not egos and personalities.	
I give people opportunities to show initiative and don't expect perfection first time.	
When someone does something I don't approve of, I describe the behaviour, its consequences and what I would like to be different. I don't undermine or belittle or engage in character assassination.	
I let people see it is safe to disagree with me. I convey respect for differences of opinion and I don't punish dissent.	
I talk appropriately about my feelings. If I am hurt, angry or offended I say so with honesty and dignity.	
I praise in public and correct in private.	
If someone does better work than me I acknowledge it with good grace.	

Ego-free leadership statement	Self score (1–10)
If someone does better work than me and I am resentful I acknowledge my resentment and ask myself what that's about.	
I hire people who can be more successful than me.	
I let people find their own solutions where appropriate. I don't always have to be the expert.	
I don't over-manage, over-observe or over-report. I allow creativity and autonomy.	
I give people as much control as possible over their work and environment.	
I give people assignments that will stretch them personally and professionally and offer appropriate levels of support without stifling or abandoning them.	
I allow people time to think and reward intellectual and theoretical input alongside "doing".	
If I say my door is open it's open. If it's shut it's shut.	
I am accessible. People don't need to wade through layers of henchmen to reach me.	
I'll make someone a coffee. I don't have to ask my PA to do it.	
I remember people's names and something about them. Because I'm interested.	
I don't believe I need to be perfect.	
I do believe I need to know myself well.	

A STEP TOWARDS SELF-AWARENESS

What do your responses tell you about:

- your strengths
- your weaknesses
- your level of self-awareness
- your blind spots
- what drives you
- what rewards you seek at work
- your values and beliefs

If there's one thing that most psychologists and personality theorists agree on, it's that most human beings have an inordinate capacity for self-deception. We seem to be designed with an in-built self-censoring function that kicks in whenever reality threatens to overwhelm us. We have enormous capacities to edit and shape the information we receive, to make the outer world fit our inner expectations. And we have an even greater capacity to distort the messages we get from our subconscious selves to make ourselves more acceptable in our own and others' eyes.

Think about the ratings you gave yourself for each of the ego-free leadership criteria. Were you as honest as you could be or were you at some level trying to build a picture of yourself that fitted with how you thought you *should* be or *would like* to be? The higher your self-esteem the less you would have needed to create a false image. The greater your self-awareness the more accurately you would have been able to identify your strengths and weaknesses. Being ego free means being free to be more of yourself without denial, pretence or apology. Being ego free means closing the gap between what you are and what you think you ought to be. Being ego free means being authentic.

4

THE EGO-
DRIVEN
CULTURE

INSTITUTIONAL EGOTISM: WHAT'S LURKING IN THE SHADOWS?

Institutional egotism is difficult to identify and even more difficult to tackle if you don't know what you're looking for.

One of the reasons it's so difficult to identify and tackle it is that most of the clues, the signs and symptoms, effectively hide in the organisational shadow, the hidden aspect of corporate life that houses all the undiscussables, the unmentionables, the unquestionables, the covert "rules" and corporate norms that can lurk unchallenged for years.

If an ego is needy or unsatisfied it will work its own agenda. If it has an unrequited craving for power, status and recognition it will play every game in the book from sophisticated manipulation to outright bullying to satisfy that craving. Too many private, public and voluntary sector bodies are run not by their appointed leaders, but by the egos that live within them. Egos that drive agendas. Egos that work behind the scenes, often unconsciously, beyond the knowledge or awareness of their owners or the organisation. Working in the shadows. Creating and shaping corporate culture, values and norms. And because ego activity is a shadow activity, often hidden even from the perpetrator, it can be difficult to identify, to name and therefore to deal with.

INDIVIDUAL BLIND SPOTS

Individuals all have blind spots. Our blind spots, or our shadows, are homes to all the bits of ourselves we don't like, or don't want to admit to. Most of us have qualities we would like to be known for: our generosity, our kindness, our insight and intelligence, our diligence... For each of us the labels will be different, but most of us are comfortable owning a few positive attributes. Equally most of us have another set of traits that we either don't acknowledge to ourselves or wouldn't like to reveal to the outside world. Because of the cultural or religious norms we live by, many of the behaviours that emanate from the ego are relegated to the shadows. The actions that come from our cravings for power, status and recognition, will rest indefinitely in the shadows unless we make a conscious decision to take a closer look at ourselves and our motivations.

CORPORATE BLIND SPOTS

It is not just individuals that have shadow sides. Organisations have them too, but shadow-side phenomena are not discussed in company literature or depicted in organisational charts, even though they permeate and influence all aspects of organisational life: strategy, operations, structure, management and leadership. Think of all the unwritten rules, the cultural norms and values, the unexamined and undiscussed "facts" that go unchallenged. If the ego wants somewhere to hide, no better place than the corporate shadow.

Everyone knows that all sorts of ego-driven activities take place behind the scenes in organisations:

- deals are struck
- reputations are ruined
- board level bullying pervades
- rules are flouted
- in-groups flourish
- out-groups become marginalised
- the innocent are blamed
- the guilty are promoted

Most of the time nothing is said. Defensive routines proliferate as people keep themselves in the dark about their own and others' shortcomings. Leaders put a gloss on their own poor performance or turn a blind eye to keep the peace rather than cause a disturbance or create conflict they might not have the skill or the emotional capacity to handle. Shadow activities generate significant costs in psychological, social and financial terms, but most of the time they go undiscussed and therefore stay outside the reach of normal managerial intervention. Activities that can substantially affect both productivity and the quality of work life in the company are glossed over and left to fester in the hope that they will just go away. They never get a hearing in the forums where something can be done about them. Egos stay protected and the culture becomes riddled with pretence and denial.

TRUTHS

Think about some of the espoused "truths" that abound in your place of work. The beliefs, values and norms that are pumped out from on high. They might look something like this:

- people are our greatest asset
- everyone gets a say
- we value everyone, regardless of age, gender or race
- mistakes are learning opportunities
- managers have an open-door policy
- we reward innovation and initiative

Are these statements a reflection of what's *really* going on, or are they being transmitted simply to protect individual empires or keep the corporate brand intact? If you scratched the surface and delved into the depths of the organisational shadow, you might find another set of hidden truths that looked more like this:

- people are expendable
- you're only heard if you tow the company line
- we only do success
- failure isn't an option
- the fittest survive
- if you mess up, hide
- if you want to speak to a manager you'll have to wait for a five minute window in his busy diary
- find out what's in your boss's mind and do it

So what keeps the discrepancy, the hypocrisy in its place? What is it in the system that enables the shadow side of organisational life to thrive and institutional egotism to flourish? What's hiding in the shadows in *your* place of work?

LOOKING BEYOND THE BRAND

What does an egotistical corporate culture look like? What are the signs, symptoms and clues that give it away? How do you know if the way you do things in your place of work is primarily and unhelpfully ego-driven?

There are many different manifestations of ego-driven culture, some obvious, some less so. Sometimes the brand image is a give-away, sometimes merely an unintentional, but effective mask hiding what's really going on underneath. Whether you are part of an international PLC or a small voluntary sector body your brand image, the outward-facing entity that you display to the world will say something about you. But as we shall see it may hide as much as it reveals.

THE ENTRANCE HALL

You can glean a certain amount about an organisation's culture just by walking into its foyer, its entrance hall, or its front office. Recently a group of researchers set about examining how much you could ascertain about an organisation's culture by doing just that: walking into its foyer. And noticing. Seeing. Hearing. Feeling. Getting a sense of the place. Chatting to its front-line staff. The researchers spent a maximum of fifteen minutes in each foyer, logged their findings then checked them out against findings produced by another, more conventional, cultural diagnostic tool. The findings were remarkable. The parity between the sense check and the conventional check surpassed all expectations.

Walk into the foyers of the big international players in the world of professional consultancy, whether it be lawyers, investment bankers or accountants and you can smell the delicious aroma of ego. Marble, glass, leather, high ceilings exude not just confidence, but raw arrogance. They are all justifiably proud of their hard-won reputations for professional excellence and corporate integrity, but what is it like to work in these proud, competitive, often brutal environments?

IMAGE IS EVERYTHING

In order to survive in a competitive market these firms vie with each other to recruit and retain the best staff and the best clients. And in order to attract both good graduates and experienced professionals they each strive to be seen as a good employer. The espoused desire to create a good working environment is given a high profile in their recruitment literature and is afforded prominence in the marketing material sent to potential clients. After all, who wants to do business with a draconian employer even if it does deliver the goods?

But take the lid off some of these prestigious firms and you will see something quite shocking. Bullying. Public ridicule. Arrogance.

ONLY THE FITTEST SURVIVE

So what do you need to *do*, what do you need to *be*, in order to gain entry and survive in many of these businesses? You need confidence certainly. Preferably arrogance. You need professional excellence. That's a given. You won't get past the first paper sift without relevant academic qualifications and a demonstrable potential for winning new contracts and bringing vast sums of money into the business. But beyond that? In an environment where everyone is scrambling for promotion physical and emotional resilience is essential. You work long hours not just to get the job done but to prove that you are committed and that the job comes first. Emotionally you need a thick skin. If you make a mistake you're unlikely to be offered the opportunity to talk it through and learn from your experience. It is much more likely that someone will delight in having detected a weakness in you. Determination is key. Not just to win new business but to stay alive and thrive within the corporate culture. If you are ever going to make it to partner you will need to demonstrate that your personality fits. And that means massaging the egos of those above you. It means saying "yes it would be a pleasure to work this weekend", not "I'm due to be best man at my brother's wedding". It means keeping quiet when you know you're right. Of course you have to maintain professional standards of integrity and a code of conduct. If you do something wrong beware. Your career will come to an abrupt and untimely halt. But it's as much about showing that you are loyal and supportive of those higher up the corporate ladder. They are always right.

Above all you have to get noticed. Everything you say has to have weight and value. Indeed it has to have *more* weight and value than your colleague's contribution. This isn't a culture of support and collaboration. This is "mind out of the way I'm coming through". Don't thank people and don't expect thanks. Don't ask, demand. This is about unadulterated ambition. You do a fantastic job and you fight for the rewards you think you deserve. Find an internal senior sponsor who will champion your cause. Curry favour with those who will put you forward for promotion. If you're going to make it to the top you need the backing of the biggest egos in the business.

PEOPLE HANG ON TO RESOURCES AND POWER

In the ego-driven culture, scarcity pervades. There is never enough to go round: money, status, recognition, reward, power, high-profile positions. The hierarchy is multi-layered to ensure that everyone is kept keen and eager for promotion. To get any sort of financial bonus you have to not only bend over backwards, but be seen to enjoy the contortion. People vie for scraps of power. They exhaust themselves in the effort to be noticed and to get their own needs met. They give every last ounce of themselves to their job. Of course they have choice. They could leave. So what keeps them working within a culture that many would regard as professional, yet upon close scrutiny reveals itself to be brutal and exploitative? Some of them, of course, are there primarily to get what they can for themselves. To get their own needs met for power, status and recognition. They may or may not have consciously weighed up the personal, domestic and health costs attached to this way of operating, but they have made a decision that they are in it for the long haul. Others enjoy the financial rewards and many the intellectual stimulation and the satisfaction that comes with delivering a good quality, highly-valued service. What is tragic is that very few of them appear to have paused to ask, "Isn't there another way?" Even if they have asked, it is doubtful many would believe they had the power to influence and change the culture from within. Even if they wanted to.

HIDDEN TRUTHS AND THE PSYCHOLOGICAL CONTRACT

So what might the hidden truths be in these prestigious firms? The truths that you won't find written in the company literature or spoken of in the boardroom?

- we're all in it for ourselves
- mistakes are ridiculed
- sycophancy is more important than respect
- only the powerful survive
- home life is an interruption to work

The unspoken truths are more influential in shaping the psychological contract between employer and employee than the spoken ones. The psychological contract is the "deal" that is struck between employer and employee and embraces all the mutual obligations that they have towards each other. It is often informal and imprecise, generated over the years through promises and implicit expectations. It is rarely articulated and not strictly enforceable, although courts may take it into account when settling a legal dispute. It is about perception, hope, expectation.

In an ego-free environment the psychological contract is built on mutual trust and confidence. Employees believe they will be:

- treated well
- dealt with fairly
- heard
- respected

In most businesses, the power brokers, the leaders and managers, like to be seen to be fulfilling their side of the bargain by providing:

- pay commensurate with performance
- opportunities for training and development
- opportunities for promotion
- recognition for innovation or new ideas
- feedback on performance
- interesting and challenging tasks
- attractive benefits packages
- respectful treatment
- job security
- a pleasant and safe working environment

However, in an ego-driven culture, with its pockets of power and its game-playing, the contract becomes biased and distorted, favouring those who are striving to protect their empires and keep themselves safe from attack or annihilation.

In the ego-driven culture the psychological contract between employer and employee could be described as being about:

- win/lose
- obedience and compliance
- manipulation
- working the system
- outputs vs job satisfaction
- inflexibility
- limited autonomy
- low levels of trust
- lack of respect

At a primitive level this is a fight for survival. Although unspoken and unwritten the psychological contract can be a force that keeps employees firmly in place and at the mercy of those who wield the power.

Not all professional consultancies operate with such brutality. Those that have the courage to scrutinise their cultural norms and practices may well find they wish to change little about the way they go about their business. Maybe the culture in which they operate does bear close examination and maybe they truly have something to shout about. However, if they are left feeling uncomfortable, or perhaps indignant, maybe they just need to look a little more closely and ask one or two outrageous, challenging questions about the way things are done.

EGOS DRIVEN UNDERGROUND

The following case study shows how an ostensibly healthy workplace culture can be distorted, infected and undermined by the ego needs of one powerful individual in the system. In many ways this example is less brutal, but nonetheless powerful because it shows what can happen when the unspoken, unacknowledged shadow-side of organisational life goes unchallenged.

This study is set in the voluntary sector, in a faith-based organisation. A charity with a strong Christian ethos wherein employees give their all because they believe in its cause and support its aims and values. People are not recruited for their raw ambition or their desire to be seen as the best. They are recruited largely for their desire to contribute to a cause beyond themselves. Not only is it undesirable to be ego-driven. In this environment it's not ok to *have* an ego. Ego needs are very definitely part of the shadow. They are unspoken, unacknowledged. In an organisation where there is a strong ethos of altruism people are not allowed to ask "what's in it for me?". They ask "how can I contribute?", "what can I give?". What they want as individuals is deemed to be unimportant. Ego needs are suppressed. People don't put themselves forward, don't overtly seek reward, recognition and status, don't forcefully champion their own goals, ideas and ambitions.

Whereas in the big consultancy firms you can sense the egos as you walk through the door, in this faith-based charity, as in many other voluntary sector organisations, ego needs are stringently denied. That's not to say they are not powerful and potentially destructive. But there is a great reluctance to acknowledge their existence. A denial that manifests in a marked resistance to tackling the fall out.

CARLA: CONTAMINATION OF THE SYSTEM

People are human and ego needs will out. Carla was a senior manager in this charity. She was charming, effusive and a skilled media communicator. When the charity needed someone charismatic and eloquent to champion its cause, Carla would be wheeled out to front the cameras and give the journalists their quotes. No one questioned that her motives were good. She put her heart and soul into her work and would work evenings and weekends to ensure that the job got done. Work on *her* causes. Issues that *she* deemed to be important. Carla had a way of ensuring that that *her* pet causes were the ones that were given prominence, funding and resources. Her concerns were the ones that made it to the top of the corporate agenda and woe betide anyone who tried to challenge her. Carla would take up inordinate amounts of space at strategy meetings. Her presentations were beautifully presented with elaborate PowerPoint illustrations. She would argue her case passionately and emotionally. And if anyone dared challenge or question her reasoning she would sulk, pout, become "unwell", or simply dig her heels in and insist that things were done her way. Carla developed a skill for blocking or undermining other initiatives that might divert resources from her own causes. In meetings inordinate amounts of time were spent keeping her happy, giving her space, paying lip service to her ideas. Ideas that were often good, but needed modification or the consideration of a broader perspective that she was invariably unwilling to concede.

People at all levels of the organisation found themselves

treading warily in her presence. They found themselves giving her more time and energy than they would afford other people. They went out of their way to show they were listening to her. They were polite. They reassured and supported her. They became fearful of challenging her lest her temper and outbursts took up even more time than she was already claiming. At every strategy meeting someone unquestioningly took on the role of Keeping Carla Happy. Someone in the senior team would get her coffee. Another would save her the best seat. They would spend time thinking about how they would present their ideas in ways that would not confront or upset her. They worried about whether she was comfortable, what she thought and felt.

Carla's behaviour infected the culture. Robust, intelligent senior figures became wary of confrontation for fear of the space and emotional energy the encounter would require. During emergencies, when her knowledge and expertise were sorely needed to deliver what was needed to people in crisis, they would tread especially carefully knowing that a false word or an unintentional challenge would cause her to hang on to her power and delay making a timely decision. Middle managers trod carefully and began huddling in corners looking over their shoulders, telling tales of Carla's latest outburst. Agendas became hidden or distorted in an effort to get round the obstacle that was Carla. One senior figure described the culture as that of a dysfunctional family, with all the deceit and manipulation that accompanies it.

For the period of her tenure in the role Carla's need for power, status and recognition drove not just her, but the entire organisation. In her attempts to shore up her position and keep herself safe, Carla had appointed people around her who were not necessarily professionally able, but who would protect her from criticism and scrutiny. What had been a business known for collaboration, debate and sound value-based judgements became toxic, fearful, lacking confidence in its ability to deliver. It became the norm to strike covert deals rather than engage in open debate. Fiefdoms began to be established as people felt a need to protect their own patch and ring-fence their resources. Managers hung onto their power and became reluctant to delegate decision making for fear of "getting it wrong". People began to think very carefully about where they placed their allegiances.

NO LANGUAGE TO TACKLE THE PROBLEM

In this organisation there was no language to tackle the problems that Carla was creating. Over a period of years the system silently adapted itself to her needs, her demands. She was never openly tackled about the difficulties her behaviour was creating. Nor indeed did anyone take her aside to listen to her personal story, find out what made her tick or what she needed to make her professional role personally fulfilling. People rarely join organisations with the intention of causing trouble or being difficult, but when a gap opens up between personal needs and corporate values someone or something in the system needs to be in place to tackle the fall out of the discrepancy. In this case Carla's need for power, recognition and status were at odds with the charity's altruistic values. This may or may not have been evident at the outset. Recruitment and selection interviews often focus primarily on the hard skill sets and give little attention to exploring the parity between personal and corporate aims and values. This organisation had ostensibly good, sound corporate aims and values that had served it well for many years. But denial of ego needs in the system, in this case embodied in one individual but undoubtedly present in other employees, caused personal pain and corporate havoc. No-one dealt effectively with Carla and all that she represented. Everyone hoped she would go away, which eventually she did of her own accord.

However the legacy of her seven-year tenure was another three to sort out the damage.

HIDDEN CULTURAL AND SOCIAL NORMS

All organisations have their own cultural and social norms. The way things are done and the way people relate to people. These norms are never published or openly acknowledged. But whether they are espoused or hidden they are a powerful force.

In an ego-driven organisation the hidden cultural and social norms are set up to ensure that someone or something is kept safe. Hidden cultural and social norms protect individuals, empires, ambitions and power. As we have seen in the last two examples, in an ego-driven culture defence mechanisms abound. You will see repression, projection, displacement, rationalisation and regression manifesting in numerous ways on a daily basis. Most of these behaviours and manifestations are either so deeply embedded in the culture or so vehemently denied that they go unnoticed. They remain so effectively hidden in the corporate shadow that for the most part they remain unidentified, unchallenged and undiscussed.

NAMING BUT NOT SHAMING

Exposing some of what lurks in the corporate shadow can be liberating, energising and productive. Leaders who have the courage and self-awareness to examine and challenge some of the behaviours, norms and expectations infecting their corporate culture are potentially unlocking a door to even greater success and profitability than they already experience. What if the power brokers in the consultancy firms had the insight to do that? What if the senior figures in the charity dared to name the dysfunctional norms setting seed in the system? What more might they achieve if they allowed themselves to be free of their hidden constraints?

SYMPTOMS OF THE EGO-DRIVEN CULTURE. HOW YOU KNOW WHEN YOU'RE IN ONE

Most organisations hide the bits of themselves they don't like, that don't support the brand image they want to convey. We have examined two examples of ego-infested cultures. What might you find lurking in the shadows of your organisation? What are the clues, the traits that might signal a need for concern, a need for action? Research across the private, public and voluntary sector organisations revealed a diverse and alarming range of unspoken, unchallenged signs and symptoms that kept ego in its place, reigning supreme. What are the great unmentionables in your business that allow egos to proliferate and stifle excellence?

HOW TO RECOGNISE AN EGO-DRIVEN CULTURE

Great Men Rule

In the ego-driven organisation Great Men rule. Historically Great Men, in times of hardship and difficulty, will come and resolve problems through a combination of strength of will, self-confidence and great intelligence. These Great Men think of themselves as powerful, influential and self-important. They believe themselves to be the ones who can and should solve all organisational ills.

Leaders selected according to outward show of strength

In the overtly ego-driven culture leaders and managers are singled out early on in their careers for demonstrating self-confidence, assertiveness, self-belief and determination. Self-confidence is held to be an effective facet of leadership in the ego-driven culture, but little credence is attached to self-awareness or self-monitoring so leaders have a tendency towards arrogance, self-absorption and aggression.

Interpersonal insensitivity is the norm

Little heed is paid to recognising or responding to the emotional needs of others. Time spent listening is thought to be time wasted unless it is to hear views and opinions that support a personal agenda. There is little empathy shown when dealing with colleagues and staff. Putting others at ease is an expendable luxury.

People hide behind uniforms and lifestyle

Uniforms might be regulation, office issue as in the police or armed forces, or the informal uniform often worn by young high flyers in corporate life. In order to be seen and to have credibility you have to wear the right label, dress in a particular way and frequent the right bars and restaurants.

People are too busy (and important) to stop and speak

Technology is one of the greatest supporters of the "too busy to stop and speak" culture. The mobile that can't be turned off, the e-mail ("I had hundreds waiting for me when I got back...") that must be answered now. People let it be known that they are doing Very Important Jobs and can't possibly create even a small window in their busy working day for anything other than Very Important Discussions.

No work-life balance

Presenteeism is the order of the day. You have to be in first and out last if you are to maintain credibility. People vie to be seen to be doing the longest hours, work the most weekends. It's about quantity not quality. Inputs not outputs.

Glory is for the chosen few

There isn't enough kudos to go round so what little there is has to be distributed carefully and sparingly. Only the chosen few can be victorious. Self-promotion is rife and scrabbling for resources is part of the working day.

Fiefdoms reign supreme

Leaders become territorial and will do all they can to protect their own patch which might be open to invasion and annihilation from every quarter. Good staff are poached. Henchmen are recruited. Foul play is hidden beneath a thin veneer of decency. Kings reign supreme over their personal courts.

Success is spectacular but temporary

With all the charm, energy, drive and charisma that egos generate, successes can be high profile and high impact. But with the motivation for success coming from individual needs seeking immediate gratification there is little incentive to leave a legacy of success for others to pick up.

Flavour of the month

There will be a culture of favouritism and the identity of these favourites will change from day-to-day, month to month. There will be in-groups and out-groups.

Goals set to further individual ambition

There is a tendency for individuals to champion causes that will further their own ambitions. People will cherry-pick initiatives that will give them more power, raise their status and enhance their profile.

In describing the culture in one university a senior academic said: "there is no sense of team work or corporate identity. We are a department of fifty individuals who happen to be in the same building and come under the same subject heading. Mostly the people working within the department see it as a home from which to base their individual activities. There's no sense of working with or for each other. Neither is there much healthy competition. Everyone is working at such an atomistic level. The culture is individualistic. Everyone wants to close their doors and get on with their own thing. To the extent that when we are putting together a strategic research plan for the department we start with what research people are doing and construct the plan from that. Not the other way round. In order to keep everyone happy and be inclusive. So we don't start with the interests of the Research Council or what our students – the customers – want to be taught. You can't do that with academics. You can't say we need research on *this*. They just won't do it. They make their own interests fit with the external need. To anyone from the outside world it's a strange way of working. It's all about egos. There's a certainty with each individual academic that their work is the most important thing. They know best. It's their right to set priorities. It is a very privileged world".

Toxic relationships proliferate

Back-scratching, sycophancy, avoidance of conflict or confrontation for fear of retribution. Distorted, inauthentic relationships permeate the culture and become the norm.

Name, shame and blame

In the ego-driven culture it's never *my* fault. The imperative is to do what ever it takes to shift the blame and reveal *someone else's* shortcomings. Projection and denial are commonplace.

Little authentic debate

Egos drive agendas. Charisma takes precedence over authenticity and pragmatism. No-one challenges the power brokers so there's no authentic debate. Good ideas are buried as self serving deals are struck.

People development is given low priority

In a me-centred culture the development of others is seen as a threat. The thinking is "if others do well they will outshine and overtake me". It is impossible to create a coaching culture with big egos running the show. Big egos don't have the awareness or the inclination to foster a coaching climate. They rely on a system of instruction and punishment to keep themselves safely in place.

Targets set to enhance image

Targets are set to make the company and the power brokers look good. In the public sector this starts with national targets designed to make the Government look good in the eyes of the public. Across health and education and the police, targets are being set that are quantitative and image-enhancing rather than qualitative and life-enhancing. One police chief spoke with regret of the driving pressure to solve crimes to make the figures look good. A pressure that made it difficult to justify putting resources into supporting the victims of crime. Spending an hour with an elderly woman who has been mugged does not enhance the statistics so is inevitably given lower priority than nailing the perpetrator.

Nepotism rules

Normal recruitment and selection procedures are bypassed and staff development and progression is a sham. Cronies are appointed and promoted and become difficult to remove or challenge in an environment that protects their interests.

Between 1993 and 2003 there were eight major reviews of corporate governance in the UK, culminating with the Higgs Report which reviewed the Role and Effectiveness of Non-Executive Directors. The UK is now regarded as having the highest standards of corporate governance in the world.

However, recent research into board effectiveness highlights a tendency amongst large companies to select non-executive directors either because they are known to the chair or because they already have board-level experience and are therefore *assumed* to be of the calibre and status required to fill the role. Headhunters often reinforce this stereotype when they select potential candidates.

Fear of disruption lies behind this tendency. Boards are highly protective of their status and image and are careful to appoint according to a known formula in order to maintain their culture. Unity is valued more highly than diversity.

Egos inhibit collaboration

In one internationally recognised PLC the board members at the London HQ all have their offices on the top floor. Ostensibly this is to ease communication and information sharing. But it takes more than close proximity of offices to bring about collaborative working when egos are at stake. On first joining the company a senior advisor to the business assumed that, if diaries permitted, briefing the team would simply be a matter of bringing them all together to share information. It wasn't just diaries that got in the way of that plan. Each of them made it clear that they wanted an individual briefing on each major new initiative. None of them was willing to risk exposure to peers until they were fully informed. None of them wanted to enter into open debate until they had been able to digest new information and evaluate it in the light of their own agendas.

Nothing changes

In the ego-driven organisation it can be difficult to drive through change when too many self-serving interests are being accommodated by keeping things as they are.

Institutional defensiveness

There will be marked avoidance of anything that challenges the status quo or threatens to undermine those with power and authority. Anyone coming in from outside who tries to hold a mirror up to the organisation and reflect back its shortcomings will be marginalised, threatened or scapegoated. One egotistical board member of an international retailing company commented, "We take great delight in chewing up consultants and spitting them out".

Cynicism abounds

Cynics – the ones who have given up but not shut up – have an uncanny ability to sniff out what's going wrong and exaggerate it. But because their own egos are fragile they are reluctant to expose *themselves* to challenge and ridicule. Their protests are made in ways that are indirect, smug and critical. Anyone who wants to change things for the better is belittled, ridiculed and berated for caring.

There's always an excuse

Mistakes in the egotistical culture are not learning opportunities. They are opportunities to rationalise, to explain away poor performance or unhelpful behaviour. Egos must be protected at all costs.

Conflict is hidden rather than open

Ego-driven managers and employees addicted to defensive routines do not always say what they mean, but will deny this skilfully when challenged. They pretend to engage in open communication, but in difficult situations will baulk at giving an honest opinion or unwelcome feedback. They may not be aware that they are avoiding conflict with others, but by doing so they wreak organisational havoc.

> Conflict that is continually left unaddressed is ultimately debilitating for the organisation and eats away at the fabric of the culture. Denial may offer a short-term reprieve, but it cannot provide a long-term answer.

JAMES: A WORD ON DENIAL

James was the CEO and founder of a small engineering company. Seventy people in all from shop floor to boardroom. James was passionate about the business. He and a friend had set it up from scratch ten years ago and from early on it had shown every sign of thriving. But gradually, over the years, James noticed that profits were not as high as he had reasonably expected. Staff turnover began to increase as good people were poached by rival businesses offering better incentives and glossier benefits packages. Materials started to go missing, rival factions and small, locally-led empires started to emerge. Communication began to break down. The design team weren't talking to the shop floor. The shop floor had little time for the sales reps. Accounts didn't trust facilities management. And so it went on. As the empires grew the egos flourished. Self-appointed spokesmen in each of the rival groups gained power and status. Stories were told and banal tales fuelled the hostility and rivalry.

As the bank became more and more concerned at the company's figures, James's stress levels rose. How could the business he had nurtured so carefully be taking a nosedive? With such capable committed people how could he fail?

Of course he knew that there was a "bit of banter" between different departments. Nothing serious though, he was sure of that. Until one of the young women in accounts threatened action against one of the design team for sexual harassment and bullying. And a long-term member of the design team was overheard telling his brother in a rival firm details of a new product that was about to hit the market. Departments became battlegrounds with internal conflict and departmental rivalry escalating.

James was stunned. Hadn't he always treated people well? Didn't he generously reward their performance and their loyalty? Hadn't he got the IIP badge on the wall to prove how people-focused the company was? Yes, but egos had infiltrated the system and were wreaking havoc.

James had completely failed to detect what was going on under his nose, in the shadows of the organisation. The competition and rivalry, the backbiting and aggression had passed him by. He expected others to be as unconditionally committed to the business as he was.

James was well intentioned but naïve when it came to the human energy and dynamics that lay beneath the surface. If you couldn't touch it or measure it he wasn't terribly sure that it was important. James's business eventually went into receivership, not because he lacked great ideas or a ready market, but because he could not acknowledge and deal with what was going on in the shadows of his own organisation. He was fuelling corporate denial, a shadow activity that had slowly but surely strangled his business. His naivety and denial cost him his life's dream.

5

MANAGING YOUR OWN EGO

IF YOU ARE EGO-DRIVEN YOU MAY NOT WANT TO READ THIS CHAPTER

If you are ego-driven you may resist the idea that you have anything to learn about yourself. You may reject the notion that anyone could tell you anything that you do not already know or shed any useful light on the way you operate.

If you are ego-driven you may:

- have allowed the trappings of power to convince you that you are invincible
- shun or ridicule the idea that you are being driven by something out of your awareness and therefore out of your control
- have come to believe in your own grandiosity
- isolate yourself from any personal feedback that might threaten your self-image
- be unable to read your own emotions and recognise their impact

The language I have used here is deliberately challenging. It is not meant to be gratuitously critical. But if you *are* blindly driven by your ego you probably won't know it or admit it to yourself.

One executive at Oracle in describing his egotistical CEO Larry Ellison said: "the difference between God and Larry is that God does not believe he is Larry". Could this be you?

A SENSE OF PERSPECTIVE

The bigger the ego the smaller the sense of perspective. If leaders allow themselves to be seduced by the trappings of success – the big cars, private jets, sycophantic attendance – they may eventually come to suffer such degrees of self-delusion that they lose their grip on reality. They may eventually believe that they deserve the deference, the luxury, the special treatment. And that others do not. Without a robust network of friends and colleagues to help them maintain a healthy perspective they can develop a potentially devastating overconfidence and risk isolation.

It isn't just high-profile, super-salaried individuals who succumb to self-delusion. Most leaders like to have the positive images they have of themselves reflected back. They don't question the deferential feedback they are given by their closest colleagues. Colleagues who are often keen to praise and defend the person on whom their career or livelihood depends. So the cycle of ingratiation and sycophancy unfolds and the emperor comes to believe he really is wearing fine new clothes.

STAYING GROUNDED AS YOU RISE THROUGH THE CORPORATE HIERARCHY

As leaders rise through the corporate hierarchy they may spend less time monitoring their environments and may pay less attention to their critics, even when those critics are well-intentioned and fundamentally supportive. In the extreme they become isolated and defended against reality. They stop listening to "bad news". When trouble is brewing and people try to alert them to potential danger the ego-driven leader will block out the message or punish the messenger, because acknowledgement of a problem could expose their fragile ego to dissent, ridicule or criticism.

As a leader, or as an individual at any level in corporate life, it can become difficult to stay grounded and in tune with your surroundings. It is all too easy to become detached from who you really are and become simply a reflection of the images that those around you hold up. If your ego is being amply fed by your followers, that is, if your needs for power, status and recognition are being fuelled by your henchmen, you are unlikely to look elsewhere for nourishment.

Some of the greatest leaders, both historic and current, are those that have the capacity to set their egos aside. They seek out (and give) positive feedback and they remain open to criticism, but without rendering themselves vulnerable to personal attack. Chris Robinson, CEO at CHASE Children's Hospice Service epitomises ego-free leadership and is clear about his philosophy. He says:

"I strive to relax and be myself. I let my values be reflected in what I do, but I don't believe it's right to put my own interests first. When people criticise me, I listen, I look for any justification in their comments, but I also recognise that what they are describing is not about *me*. It's about the part of me they have experienced. I try not to let others set my standards for me. I am always open to improvement, but I separate personal attack from constructive criticism. I do try to keep my ego out of the way. If your ego plays a central role in all you do then you become vulnerable and you make bad decisions. In this role it's CHASE that matters. Not me."

SELF-DEVELOPMENT: YOUR CHOICE

Whatever you are trying to achieve, whether it be understanding another individual better or freeing yourself from the tyranny of your own ego – becoming ego free, the start point is *you*. We are all a work in progress. None of us is perfect or completely sorted out, emotionally or psychologically. We all have work to do; baggage to unpack, demons to be faced.

Whether you choose to do the work is up to you. No-one can force you to embark on a journey of self-discovery. No-one can make you stick with it. You might be sent on the most expensive, prestigious development programme the market can provide, but if you are physically present and emotionally absent you will learn nothing. Only you can determine how deeply you delve and which routes you take to your, perhaps as yet unclear, personal destination. Whether you opt for coaching, counselling, psychometric testing, tailored personal or leadership development programmes, a self-managed learning group or a period of reflection, only *you* can define a successful outcome. Only *you* can know what you want to learn and why you want to learn it. Only *you* can decide whether you are going to engage in the process or ignore it. Only *you* will know what developing self-awareness means to you.

Whether you are a leader, a manager or a colleague, operating with self-awareness and a solid foundation of self-esteem is key in determining personal satisfaction and business success. Inauthentic, ego-driven individuals who lack awareness of their own drives and behaviours create toxic, unproductive work environments. If you don't know, trust and respect yourself you cannot know, trust and respect others. You cannot build meaningful relationships or have authentic dialogue with those around you. If you don't know, trust and respect yourself you cannot lead.

BUILDING SELF-ESTEEM

Ego-free individuals have higher levels of self-esteem and self-awareness than those who are ego-driven. Although egotists can *appear* to be confident and robust, this outward display of bravado can often mask a deep-seated insecurity or fear of being exposed as somehow unworthy.

If you have high self-esteem you have a fundamental confidence in your ability to cope with the challenges of life – you know that you are worthy of happiness and respect.

Our level of self-esteem impacts on everything we do. If we have high self-esteem we will:

- set ourselves challenging goals
- feel happy in the presence of confident people
- not be threatened by others' success
- forgive ourselves when we mess up

If we have high self-esteem we have resistance, strength, a capacity to bounce back after a knock. We will put our energies into seeking out joyful experiences rather than constantly striving to avoid pain. If we believe in ourselves, the world is a safe, welcoming place and we have no need to hide behind an egotistical mask that scares off the enemy.

Building self-esteem isn't about surrounding yourself with people who tell you what you want to hear. That's about building an image.

Building self-esteem is about:

- building in time for reflection
- listening to feedback
- having the courage to look beyond the image you have created to discover your own intrinsic worth and value
- relieving the sycophants of their duties
- being clear what you believe – about yourself and those around you
- articulating and living by your values

Creating space for reflection may be a challenge. It may be at odds with a personal or corporate belief that everyone has to be *doing* something all the time. Roderick M Kramer spent time studying bold, high-flying executives who dazzle everyone with daring and flair, only to commit what he describes as stunning acts of folly just when they seem to have it all. Why do so many leaders, he asks, display remarkable adroitness while courting power – but crash and burn once they've secured it? The pursuit of power changes people in profound ways, he suggests. To get to the top, people often feel compelled to jettison the same attitudes and behaviours – such as modesty, prudence and self-restraint – that they'll need for survival once they've achieved the apex. But not all successful executives, he says, fall victim to the genius-to-folly syndrome. Those who make it to the top – and stay there peacefully – all share a remarkable sense of proportion and a high degree of self-awareness, despite widely differing personalities and management styles.

Writing in the *Harvard Business Review* Kramer goes on to note that whilst leaders intellectually embrace the notion of reflective leadership, reflection is often undervalued in corporate life:

> "Successful leaders strive to become more reflective. That's paradoxical given that today's business culture celebrates action over hesitancy. Americans in particular admire leaders who break new ground, transform industries and smash glass ceilings. Given this overemphasis on *doing,* it's not surprising that many of the fallen leaders I studied appeared to have a strikingly impoverished sense of self and remain curiously oblivious to many of their own tendencies that expose them to risk."

BUILDING SELF-AWARENESS: LIVING CONSCIOUSLY

Building self-awareness means learning to trust yourself and others. It means learning to differentiate between the "yes" men who are only in it for themselves and the critics who, with integrity and authenticity, are looking beyond themselves to create something great.

It's very easy to assume that people who appear self-confident, at ease with themselves and others, were born that way. We resort to saying or thinking "it's alright for him, he had a loving family, a good education...". And sometimes that is true. There are people who just came out that way, whose families gave them sound emotional support and encouraged them to believe in themselves. But there are as many grounded, secure individuals who have had to work at it. These are the people who at some level have made a decision to live *consciously*. They have chosen to take life's experience, good or bad and learn from it. They have chosen to take responsibility for their own worth and value. They have taken ownership of their own identity and they resist defining themselves according to other people's opinions and values.

If we live consciously we are less likely to be at the mercy of the whims of those around us. If we live consciously we decide whether or not we respond to others' demands. If we live consciously we know our own failings and foibles and we evaluate them with realism and compassion. We forgive ourselves. We live comfortably with ourselves.

If we live consciously we don't have to rely on our egos to get our needs met. We can ask clearly and assertively for what we want and we can defend ourselves adequately from real, rather than imagined threats.

Have you got what it takes to live consciously? I am not asking whether you can do it now. I am asking whether you have the will, the energy and the commitment to do the work and explore your choices and your power. If you want to build self-esteem you have to build your capacity to live consciously. If you want to build your capacity to live consciously you need to raise your self-awareness. And if you raise your self-awareness you will be able to answer the question "Who am I?" with confidence and conviction.

ARE YOU SEEN AS EGO-DRIVEN OR EGO-FREE?
INVITING FEEDBACK

One effective if challenging way to gain insight into your behaviour and its impact on those around you is to invite feedback on how they experience you. To invite such feedback requires a degree of trust both on the part of the person initiating it and the person giving it. Feedback is a powerful tool and needs to be sought and given responsibly. If you want to know whether you are seen as ego-driven then you need to be clear about why you are inviting comment. Do you genuinely want to hear what others think of you so that you can learn from it? Or will you use their comments to uncover dissenters and somehow find ways to punish those who are critical? Be clear about your intentions, both to yourself and with those involved in the feedback process. If your intentions are anything other than genuine they will leak out and people will find ways to sidestep or manipulate the process for their own protection. They might tell you what they think you want to hear. They might fail to engage. They aren't necessarily being difficult, they just might not trust or understand why you want to know their views.

Think too about how you will deal with the information you are given. What if it isn't what you expected, or what you wanted to hear? What support do you have in place to help you make sense of it? A coach? A counsellor? An experienced and trusted member of staff? If you are working with a coach discuss with him or her the wisdom of inviting feedback, why you are doing it and what you hope to achieve. Engaging in any development process needs considerable thought. Remember you will be working with the people you invite to participate long after the boxes have been ticked and the questionnaires returned.

When you decide to invite people to give you feedback try to select those who will offer it with honesty and integrity. Colleagues who will offer it in a spirit of goodwill and support. Just as you need to be clear about your intentions in inviting the feedback, you need to have some insight into their intentions in giving it.

Tell those you are inviting to participate why you are seeking their views and observations. It may be appropriate to open up a little about yourself. You may find in doing so other people become interested or begin to talk about themselves at a level deeper than that at which they usually engage. Trust your intuition. Push out the boundaries but keep yourself safe. Risk spreading a little authenticity and see what you discover. You never know, it might catch on.

How you might want to use the questionnaire

This is a tool to be used flexibly. There are a number of ways you might employ it and you may well find your own. Some possibilities might be:

- Reproduce it and give it to a number of chosen people with a few words, either written or spoken, about why you are engaging in this and when you would like it back.
- Use it as a vehicle for opening up a discussion not just about yourself, but the culture within your business or your team.

- Invite a third party to distribute it and collate the anonymous responses as you would with 360 degree feedback.
- Think about an ego-free leader you admire. Fill this in as though you were giving *them* feedback. What do you discover about how they operate and the differences between them and you?

However you decide to use it, be humble with your request for feedback. Demanding a response is rarely productive and may say something about the condition of your ego!

Peer feedback: Ego-driven or ego-free?

No.	Ego-free behavioural statement	✔ or ✗	Comment (optional)
1	Keeps promises and honours commitments. Acts with integrity		
2	Invites feedback and accepts it with good grace		
3	Learns from others, no matter what their status in the company		
4	Works effectively but not for effect. Is not a workaholic		
5	Listens more than talks		
6	Hears what people say		
7	Treats others with respect		

No.	Ego-free behavioural statement	✔ or ✗	Comment (optional)
8	Apologises when necessary		
9	Shows empathy and understanding for others		
10	Is not blaming or judgemental		
11	Sets clear, fair standards for behaviour and performance, and supports people in achieving them		
12	Does not give orders unnecessarily. Offers reason and explanation when appropriate		
13	Allows me to say "I don't know" or "I'll find out" without fear of ridicule or retribution		
14	Does not blame or ridicule me when I make a mistake		
15	Helps me see mistakes as learning opportunities		
16	Manages disputes by focusing on facts not personalities		
17	Lets people show initiative		
18	Does not expect perfection first time		
19	Allows me to disagree with his/her view without fear of retribution		

No.	Ego-free behavioural statement	✔ or ✘	Comment (optional)
20	Will talk appropriately about his/her own feelings. Does not suppress or exaggerate own emotion		
21	Corrects in private and praises in public		
22	Doesn't have to be expert. Lets people find their own solutions		
23	Does not over manage, over-observe or over-report		
24	Allows creativity and autonomy		
25	Gives people as much control as possible over their work and environment		
26	Gives people assignments that will stretch them personally and professionally		
27	Supports individuals' learning without stifling or abandoning them		
28	Allows people time to think		
29	Is accessible		
30	Remembers people's names. Is interested in them		

No.	Ego-free behavioural statement	✔ or ✘	Comment (optional)
31	Encourages people to challenge the status quo and question existing methods and strategies		
32	Puts the business agenda ahead of own agenda		
33	Discourages empires and cliques		
34	Works collaboratively with colleagues		
35	Rises above turf wars and political in-fighting		
36	Encourages leadership to flourish at all levels of the organisation		
37	Asks good questions as well as giving good answers		
38	Encourages everyone to be successful at something		
39	Responds to change initiatives according to business need vs personal need		
40	Is a confident, capable mentor		
41	Promotes personal development for self and others		

No.	Ego-free behavioural statement	✔ or ✘	Comment (optional)
42	Promotes professional development for self and others		
43	Recruits the best person for the role – not just personal supporters		
44	Empowers others		
45	Shares glory		
46	Shares power		
47	Shares knowledge		
48	Will leave a legacy of ongoing excellence		

What does this feedback tell you?

You have had the courage to invite others' views. Now what? First, take stock of how you are feeling having read the responses.

Are you:

- delighted?
- angry?
- outraged?
- surprised?
- curious?
- excited?
- keen to explore further?
- determined never to engage in such a process again?
- puzzled?
- overwhelmed?

Whatever you feel, your emotion is telling you something. If you are feeling any kind of discomfort ask yourself what that is about. Have you been confronted by your shadow, the part of yourself that you hide away and don't face? Or have you been surprised and delighted by the positive picture that those around you have painted? Right now you may well have more questions than answers.

Questions like:

- what is this telling me?
- does my way of doing things support my personal aims and values?
- is my way of operating right for the business?
- do I need to change my behaviour in any way?
- how will I build on and make the most of my positive traits?
- how can I learn more about myself?
- how do I raise my self-awareness?
- what do I need to help me?
- who will I talk to about this?

Whether you have been delighted or dismayed by the feedback you have been given take time to reflect. Let it all sink in. Decide what you are going to do with it. Be clear how you will learn from it and integrate the learning into your way of operating in your workplace and beyond.

IMD BELIEVES BIG CORPORATE PLAYERS NEED TO GET TO KNOW THEMSELVES

It's easy and perhaps tempting, to file all this self-awareness stuff away in the soft and fluffy category. A nice-to-have, but not a priority. However many of the big corporate players take a different view and are investing significant amounts of money in supporting their key people to become self-aware, authentic leaders. The corporate world is beginning to realise that intellectual ability is a necessary, but not sufficient, condition for business success and that emotional capacity is crucial to survival. IMD, the International Institute for Management Development, is one of the world's leading business schools. Based in Lausanne it has fifty years' experience in developing the leadership capabilities of international business executives. It includes amongst its clients board members from world-class corporations. In 2005 *The Wall Street Journal* ranked IMD ahead of other international business schools for its innovative and highly acclaimed MBA (Masters in Business Administration) programme.

In recent years, the IMD MBA has earned a worldwide reputation for its innovation and business relevance in a highly competitive MBA marketplace. To gain a place on the IMD MBA you don't just pay up and pitch up. You are selected according to your academic and leadership ability, your career history and, crucially, your willingness to learn about yourself. The IMD approach is less about teaching and more about creating an environment in which participants can learn, share ideas and stay open to feedback. Participants on an IMD programme do not learn about leadership by spending time in a classroom listening to gurus. They learn about leadership by undertaking real-time consultancy projects in places like Bosnia-Herzegovina, a country disrupted by conflict that is trying to get its economy back on track. This is a serious programme for serious players.

Part of the success of its MBA programme, IMD believes, is its emphasis on what it describes as *personal* leadership development, alongside *business* leadership development. Successful leaders, they say, lead from their authentic selves, from their own strengths and weaknesses and from their hearts as well as their minds. Before they start the programme each participant writes a personal inventory statement. Their assignment is to write about themselves – their strengths and weaknesses, their goals, their failings. And they must rewrite this statement three times during the course of their time with IMD as they grow in experience. Many of the participants describe this as a difficult, challenging and often unfamiliar process.

THE MBA THAT OFFERS ACCESS TO A PSYCHOANALYST

IMD's aim is to enable participants to discover, or deepen their knowledge of their authentic selves. In addition to the written personal inventory and the experiential group work, each of them has the opportunity to take a "personal development elective" which includes twenty sessions with a psychoanalyst, allowing them to deepen their self-understanding and become more effective leaders than they would otherwise be. A recent internal review of the programme concluded that this was a crucial and effective element of the MBA and was essential in developing leadership capacity that was fit for the challenges of the international arena.

Self-development is no soft option. Increasingly authenticity and self-awareness are being recognised as essential elements of leadership. This is not about cost. It is about investment. These graduates are recognised internationally as highly-trained and focused professionals who are recruited by leading companies for global roles with high level responsibility. They have displayed the courage to ask the question "who am I?" and look for the answer. They have made the decision to live consciously.

TAKING RESPONSIBILITY AND TAKING RISKS

Your development is your responsibility. You can only raise your self-awareness by consciously pushing out your personal boundaries, taking a few emotional risks and inviting feedback. Professor of Organisational Behaviour at IMD, Jack D Wood advises participants on how to get the most from their time with IMD:

Maximizing your learning during a leadership programme – like exercising leadership – requires authenticity, investment, commitment and a willingness to take certain emotional risks. The more naturally and spontaneously you behave, the more experiences you have available for your reflection and learning. Authenticity means voicing your thoughts and feelings as they occur. Investment means putting your heart into the work of learning. Commitment means leaving your heart there through good and bad moments. Risk-taking calls for moving outside your usual comfort zone.

We often begin working with a new group by asking the participants how much they would like to be challenged. More often than not, they understand the question in terms of physical challenges – with images of bungee jumping and abseiling down steep cliffs. We are, however, referring to a psychological challenge. The first critical step out of your comfort zone is not physical but emotional. This allows you to experience, express and explore emotional material that we habitually avoid, dismiss, forget, or conceal behind the comfort of formal roles and familiar routines.

In our experience – without exception – a class cannot be challenged any further than the degree to which individuals are willing to challenge themselves. Each participant possesses the capacity to explore and learn and each has the ultimate authority and responsibility to decide how deep they want to push the exploration of their own behaviour. Hence, if meaningful and long-lasting development is what you're after, it is essential that you take responsibility for shaping and discovering your own learning. You will be asked to articulate your expectations and concerns and encouraged to actively pursue whatever you wish to get out of the programme. The faculty provides a framework and several learning opportunities, but you determine what you learn, how much you learn and the pace at which you learn.

Taking responsibility is helped immeasurably by working with a sense of freedom, willingness to take the initiative, courage to explore and openness to being surprised by what you might find – as well as by the way in which you learn. Scepticism, reluctance and defensiveness are as natural and spontaneous as courage, openness and risk-taking. As long as you are willing to explore what provokes your behaviour, you will derive lasting learning from the programme and further develop your leadership capacity.

INITIATING YOUR OWN DEVELOPMENT ACTIVITY

Not everyone will have the opportunity, the need or the desire to embark upon the type of programme described here. You might decide that you want to do one or more of the following:

- work with a coach
- embark on a mentoring relationship
- take part in counselling
- undergo psychometric testing
- take part in a personal development programme
- join an action learning group
- make good use of the company's appraisal scheme

Whatever route you choose to follow on your journey towards becoming ego free, know that it's your journey. You choose what you do, when and how you do it. Go at your own pace and above all enjoy.

NOT FOR THE LIKES OF ME?

Despite having worked for many years within organisations I am still occasionally surprised by how many people still work with the "it's not for the likes of me" mentality and have no experience of, or inclination towards, discovering who they really are. We have experienced huge technological advances. We carry laptops, iPods and BlackBerries. Mostly we don't know how they work. If they go wrong we pay someone to fix them, or we discard them and move on to the next thing. So it is with our emotional and psychological make-up. Too many people know little and care less about what drives them. Maybe, if they go through a crisis, a divorce or redundancy, they pay someone to fix them, patch them up and get them going again. But how many people do you know in corporate life who spend serious time, energy and money on their own personal development? On strengthening their psychological core, rather than just mending it when it goes wrong? As with our computers, most of us access only a tiny fraction of our own capability and potential. Most of us will go through our working lives without ever finding out just how extraordinary and how able we are and how infinitely more interesting and exhilarating our lives could be if only we knew ourselves at a deeper level. If we knew what drove us forward and held us back. Most people in organisational life settle for personal mediocrity because mediocrity is unthreatening. Self-discovery can be an uncomfortable journey and there's often no identifiable destination, just a series of stops along the way to soak up a new view, revel in a new place. But not embarking on the journey leaves us static, shallow and without any hope of becoming... more.

The journeys we remember are the ones that embrace adventure and a degree of risk. You may have just started yours, or you may be a long way down the road. But wherever you are, as the ad says: Just Do It.

6

MANAGING OTHER PEOPLE'S EGOS

EGOS DEMAND ATTENTION

Working with, or managing, people with big egos can be exhausting. People with big egos demand attention and take up a lot of time and emotional space as they strive for power, status and recognition. It's not just the loud, attention-seeking individuals which take the space. The individual quietly but clearly working his own agenda will be as much of a drain on resources as his ebullient, more obviously ego-driven colleague.

Egos have an energy which, if not managed appropriately by the individual himself or those around him can wreak havoc and destruction. Most organisations set up formal and informal reward systems to ensure that employees will channel their energies to meet the needs of the customer first, their department second and themselves last. But individual egos will have other priorities and in traditionally run businesses often it is the needs of individual egos which are met first, with the department and the customer trailing in their wake.

Carla in the faith-based charity was an example of someone who sought to meet her own individual ego needs ahead of the needs of the client or the organisation. Carla's ego-energy was spent on ensuring that she got what she needed when she needed it. What we saw in that case study was a massive haemorrhaging of energy – hers and her colleagues' – away from the business and all it was seeking to achieve.

So how do we find a way of working productively with those whose ego needs drive their every move? If we are managers how do we harness that unstoppable ego-energy so that the individual, the customer and the business can all benefit? How do we deal with the colleague that causes us to tear our hair out with despair as she charges through the working day, forging ahead with her own agenda regardless of the needs or sensibilities of those around her?

IDENTIFICATION IS THE FIRST STEP

When we are in the midst of a difficult working relationship it can be difficult to formulate an effective strategy for action because quite often we do not know what we are dealing with. During the interviews I conducted in the course of researching this book many of the participants reported a weight having been lifted from their shoulders as a result of naming some of the ego-driven issues they were facing. It was as though by looking through a particular lens and thus giving some shape, structure and identity to the problem they could begin to see through the mist of confusion and gain some much-needed clarity.

One participant said: "I had never thought about this colleague being ego-driven. All I saw was a bully, a selfish insensitive character who caused me a great deal of distress. By having some understanding that she was being driven by something inside her, something she needed to protect her and keep her safe, I could begin to show some empathy and work with her with a degree of compassion. I'd never thought of her being vulnerable or fragile. I was so busy looking after myself that I suppose I never got as far as thinking about her needs. She's still a pain! But something's shifted in our working relationship and I am now finding ways to get myself heard by her. I no longer avoid her because I'm anxious or confused about her likely reaction to something I do or say".

BEHIND THE BRAVADO

Before we begin to formulate a strategy for dealing with someone else's ego it is worth thinking about what might lie behind the bravado and the brash behaviour that characterises the ego-driven individual. Beneath the surface the ego is fragile. Egotists fear that they will be overlooked, or, in the extreme, annihilated. They may be seeking reassurance that they are perfect, omnipotent, that they "own" the space around them. They may try to control the rules, the processes, the flow of events. When their sense of control is threatened they may respond as though their survival is at stake. And although it is sometimes difficult to appreciate, at a deep level they fear people who appear confident and robust and may display hurt and outrage or quickly back down.

Egotists often set very high standards, both for themselves and for those who work with them. And if you are caught up in the "trying to please them" game you may find yourself exploited as you try harder and harder, working longer and longer hours to produce enough of what they want to the standard they demand.

The underlying message that the egotist conveys is: "I can control you. You cannot stand up to me. You are weak and I am strong".

Jennifer was a bright, articulate graduate. Having been born into a family of solicitors and barristers, all her life she had set her sights on being a lawyer. But after completing a law degree Jennifer began to question her motives for wanting to follow in the family tradition and decided instead to pursue a career in HR. Still intrigued by the workings of the legal profession she decided to apply for an HR role in a prestigious firm of London solicitors.

Jennifer was confident and energetic and entered her new role with enthusiasm and commitment. As sole HR practitioner responsible for forty staff she was stimulated and challenged by the wide range of personnel issues that needed to be tackled with professionalism and sensitivity. She was happy. She had found her niche in an environment she found stimulating.

But over the months Jennifer began to feel that some of the solicitors in the practice were treating her differently from the way they treated each other. They would talk to her as though she couldn't possibly understand the levels of complexity that they handled. She felt they were talking down to her, treating her role as a "nice to have" but hardly an essential component in the life of a legal practice. One day over lunch with John, one of the more junior solicitors, she let it be known that she had graduated not just with a law degree but with a first. It was as though she had admitted to having committed a crime. From then on her relationship with John began to flounder.

more importantly, sort out my response to it. I realised I couldn't sort out John's insecurities. I think he found my confidence quite threatening and certainly when it became apparent I had a better degree than him I could see why he might have felt put out. He had struggled to get his degree and when he was offered a placement in the practice he had seen it as a significant achievement. But I think he still felt he was on trial and had to prove himself if he was going to make it as a lawyer.

I realised I needed to build a relationship of trust with John. He saw me as a threat, especially because of my ease with the senior partners. He couldn't label me or put me in a box. He saw me as being in a support role so I shouldn't have been a threat to him, but he *was* threatened. And that often manifested in quite aggressive, bullying behaviour.

My strategy was to treat him with respect. I talked to him as an adult, not as if he were an overbearing parent. And I was careful never to get caught up in a spiral of sarcasm. If he made a sarcastic comment to me it would respond in a straightforward, adult way, sometimes checking out what he meant but never with an implication that he was wrong, or – worse – stupid, which would only have undermined him all the more. I just didn't get caught up in what seemed like his game. I knew I was doing my job well and had confidence in that, so when he levelled criticism at me I would ask him to elaborate, to spell out what his often oblique statements actually meant. And I listened to his response without offering counter criticisms or defence. I heard what he said and weighed up its value as I would have done with anyone else. What I *didn't* do was suck up to him or give him more attention than I would have given to any of his colleagues.

Over time I began to notice a change in his behaviour. It started one day when he stuck his head round the door to see whether I wanted to go out for a sandwich at lunchtime. Something that hadn't happened since my 'admission' about my law degree.

We had an OK lunch. At that point he still wasn't completely comfortable with me and I was very careful not to say anything that could appear critical or threatening, even light-heartedly. A year down the line and we have found a way of working with each other that I think is a lot less stressful for both of us. I don't think we'll ever completely relax and become best buddies. We treat each other with care and respect. And gradually we seem to be understanding each other better. He can see now that I'm not vying for position with him personally or professionally and I understand that it wasn't really me he was getting at, just a type of person he thought I represented. He trusts me not to undermine him and he knows I won't criticise him behind his back. So in a sense there's almost no point in his ego acting up. It's been a tough time and learning about people has been ten times harder than learning about law".

SO WHAT WAS GOING ON?

Before tackling someone else's ego it's best to take a look at the state of your own. So in examining what was going on in this scenario let's start with Jennifer because she was the one who had identified the problem and who needed to find a solution and take action. Jennifer could be described as ego free. She had ego needs but because she was aware of them (she admitted she had been drawn towards the legal profession because of the status and prestige that went with it) she wasn't blindly driven by them. Jennifer could have answered the question "who am I"? with some clarity and depth. She had a strong sense of her own worth and value both personally and professionally and was clear about what motivated her. After working through an initial period of confusion about her deteriorating relationship with John she began to develop some considerable insight into what was going on both for her and for him.

Her apparently high levels of self-awareness and self-esteem helped her cope. She was competent in dealing with the basic challenges of life. She believed she was worthy of happiness. This supported her in identifying the problem she was facing and enabled her to stay and work with it. She neither ran away nor got caught up in the inauthentic, gamey behaviour that John displayed. She maintained an adult, respectful dialogue with him and saw the importance of building a relationship of trust so that his fragile ego was not threatened further. She tackled his criticisms with a spirit of enquiry, didn't get caught up in retaliatory behaviour and above all, maintained an attitude of respect rather than defensiveness or sycophancy. And she was realistic enough to know that she could not sort out his insecurities. The only thing she could tackle was her own attitude and behaviour.

John displayed many of the behaviours and ego defence mechanisms we associate with the ego-driven individual. His self-awareness and self-esteem appeared to be at a low level. He was threatened by Jennifer's confidence and success and dealt with that threat in ways that were gamey and manipulative. He could not articulate his doubts and fears with any insight or clarity. He engaged in projection; he couldn't admit to his own shortcomings so he was driven to highlight hers. In many ways his behaviour was regressive, acting out in a childlike way as he felt the need to "show off" his successes and engage in destructive, inauthentic behaviour that did not directly communicate what he was thinking or feeling. John was driven by his ego needs. Jennifer was informed by hers.

The healthier our self-esteem, the more inclined we are to treat others with respect, benevolence, goodwill and fairness, because we don't see others as a threat and because self-respect is the foundation of respect for others. With healthy self-esteem we don't rush to interpret relationships in adversarial terms. We don't approach our encounters with others with automatic expectations of rejection, humiliation, treachery or betrayal. If we are dealing with others' ego-driven behaviour we need first to pay attention to our own ego needs.

HOW MIGHT *YOU* MANAGE AN EGO-DRIVEN COLLEAGUE?

What can you take from Jennifer's experience? What principles and guidelines might you draw out from the other examples we have seen of ego-driven behaviour? If you are working alongside an egocentric colleague or are working for an ego-driven boss what might you try?

WORKING WITH AN EGO-DRIVEN COLLEAGUE

- hang on to your sense of self
- know who you are and what you value
- be clear about your own strengths
- be clear about your vulnerabilities – know when your own buttons are being pushed
- know who owns the problem – you!
- take responsibility for tackling it
- don't threaten
- don't succumb to sycophancy
- be consistent and sensitive
- recognise that you cannot change someone else's behaviour, only your response to it
- work on building relationships of trust
- don't gossip. Offload appropriately – not in the staff restaurant
- don't get caught up in game playing – it's easy to be sucked into spirals of sarcasm and blame
- show respect
- don't betray trust
- be adult
- be clear about the difference between irritating but permissible egotism and unacceptable bullying
- recognise when being "nice" and being compliant needs to be replaced by firmer, clearer action
- ask for clarity when offered criticism
- stay curious – explore his words and the meaning behind them without confrontation or threat
- don't become the victim. Labelling the egotist as persecutor is not productive and he may, subconsciously, fuel the unhealthy dynamic between you
- develop strong emotional boundaries. He is not your friend
- beware the "informal chat to sort everything out"
- create your own physical and emotional space and be clear when he is invading it
- work on developing your tolerance of frustration, ambiguity and anxiety
- take time to renew your energy. Stand back. Take a break. Dealing with egotism can be debilitating
- know when to stop trying

DEALING WITH EGO-ENERGY IN THOSE YOU MANAGE

As a manager you have a choice. You can liberate the ego-energy in those you manage. Or you can frustrate it. If you yourself are fairly ego free you will be more likely to have the confidence to liberate it. If you are ego-driven you are more likely to be influenced by your own need for power and status and will at some level feel threatened by others' attempts to claim some of your space. No matter how much you understand intellectually your responsibility to motivate and manage others for the greater good of the organisation, you cannot bypass your "self". You cannot ignore the question "who am I?" in the context of your business.

ROGER: A LEGACY OF LIBERATION

Roger was passionate about laundries. He could talk laundries from sunrise to sunset. As managing director of a well-known laundry chain he would travel the country inspecting sites, ensuring that all was well within his empire. When he took over as MD the chain was making a loss and staff turnover was higher than you would expect, even for an industry with a transient workforce. By the time he left profits were at an all-time high and labour turnover had dropped to 10%, rendering it amongst the best in the industry. But his legacy went beyond profit and turnover. His was a legacy of liberation.

Roger had gone into the laundry business at sixteen as an administrative trainee. He had a keen mind, was willing to learn and he was ambitious. Over the years his insight and business acumen ensured that he moved rapidly through the supervisory and managerial hierarchy, securing more responsible roles and greater accountability. Finally he gained the most senior appointment, managing director, with all that went with it: the car, the office, the PA, the salary.

I met Roger some years after he had been appointed MD. He had invited me in to do some coaching with his executive team and as part of my familiarisation with the business he took me on a tour of one of the laundries. What I witnessed as I walked round the site with him was inspirational.

As we moved out of Roger's office and into the corridor that separated it from the shop floor I commented on the photos lining the walls, some of which clearly dated back several decades. Noticing my interest, Roger talked me through them, charting not just the history of the site, but the people, giving names and explaining family connections.

We walked on and around the site. It became evident that this was an MD in touch not just with his business but the individuals within it. He would pause to speak to people. He knew their names, no matter where they fitted into the organisational hierarchy. He knew something about them, whether they had a son who was doing exams or a dependent elderly mother. He knew what role they filled and how long they had been in the company. And they in turn treated him with respect. They clearly knew who was in charge, but they were relaxed with him. They responded to his interest in them both as people and as members of his workforce. Those doing the most menial jobs would stop and talk freely to him about what they were doing, how it was going, what frustrations they were facing. None of these interactions took very long. This wasn't idle time-wasting chatter. It was respectful, good quality communication between a senior manager and those he clearly valued as essential members of his team.

Roger's reputation within his business and the wider sector was built both on his hard-nosed business acumen and his ability to manage people. He had the respect of his colleagues on the executive team and was sought out as a source of valuable information from people within the industry. He was no soft touch. Consistent poor performance and an unwillingness to change would mean dismissal. If one of his managers proved over time to be unable or unwilling to manage his team effectively and repeatedly failed to meet his targets he would be out. But Roger focused on the "how" as much as the "what".

ROGER'S PHILOSOPHY ON MANAGEMENT AND LEADERSHIP

Roger doesn't waste words. "You're not a leader if no-one follows you" was his opening gambit when I asked him about his philosophy on management and leadership. Roger saw himself both as a leader, driving the strategic direction of the company and a manager of people and resources.

As a leader he knew he had power to shape and influence both the business and the individuals within it and he took his responsibilities seriously in both areas. He was confident. He was at ease with himself and with others. He believed that if he was going to achieve the business successes he desired he would do better to wield his power *with* people rather than *over* them unless or until it became necessary to step in and use his authority.

One of the things that struck me early on in my dealings with Roger was his humility. He didn't believe he was always right and was happy to get another view on what he was doing if he was unsure about his tactical or strategic decisions. Even with people doing routine jobs. He explained: "If something goes wrong on the shop floor one of the first people you ask about what went wrong and how to solve it is the person doing the job. Not a manager several layers and often hundreds of miles removed. I believe that with every pair of hands comes a free brain and I want to access it all. If I'm too proud to go to that man or woman and ask them their opinion I shouldn't be in this role. If you allow your status to become a barrier they won't communicate with you. And if they won't communicate with you, you don't have all the facts you need to make the best decision. So you can't be as effective as you might be without breaking down some of the barriers".

BREAKING DOWN BARRIERS

"One of the ways to break down barriers is to spend time getting to know your staff. You have to walk the job whether you're the MD or a supervisor. You cannot lead if you're not visible, so you make yourself visible. I made a point of talking to every employee in every site throughout the year. Particularly when they were struggling, say working on a bank holiday, or dealing with the death of a colleague. I wanted them to know I understood some of what they were dealing with. And I always tried to ensure I knew the names of the people I was going to visit, especially the ones who had just joined us. I would take the staff list home with me the night before a visit – sometimes 250 people – and test myself. And when I went round the sites I talked and I listened. I talked about where the company was going and what it needed from its workforce and I listened to their views, their concerns and their insights. It's surprising what you can glean from the guy driving the van. Ultimately it makes good business sense. If I needed to ask one laundry to pull out all the stops to help another that was in trouble I could be confident they would do it because they knew I wouldn't ask them to do anything that was unreasonable or unnecessary".

So what of Roger's ego needs? "The strategy needs to be ego-driven. It has to come from the self. Someone has to want to do something and usually that something is making money. Profitability has to be one of your main goals. But you don't have to behave in a typically egocentric way to achieve your goals. Of course people want their leaders to lead. They want them to have a clear strategy and clear goals. And they like having something to aspire to. When I took on the role of MD I found it all a bit of a strain, having to take on the mantle, wear the robes and crown. At first it didn't fit. I wasn't comfortable having the Mercedes parked in the MD's parking space when everyone else was scrabbling to find a space in the side streets for their ten-year-old hatchbacks. But eventually I took it all on and shaped it to fit. I discovered that the workforce were proud to work for a company that was seen to be successful and that included being led by someone driving a decent car. Once, when I let it be known that I was thinking of opting for a perfectly serviceable but less prestigious make and model of car one of the supervisors pointed out that the workforce wouldn't like it if they thought I was less important than the other MDs!

One of my main aims was to share my strategy with everyone in the business in a way that they would understand. Once or twice I had to deal with an ego-driven line manager who wasn't prepared to share that information. They wanted to hang on to the knowledge and the power that went with it. They refused to hold regular briefing meetings. They wouldn't talk to their staff. So they had to go. The egos sitting just below the top of the organisation can be bigger than the ones at the top and if they're causing problems you have to take action".

UNDERSTANDING IS KEY

Understanding some of what drives the person with the big ego is a key step in formulating a strategy for action. By now you will have an understanding of what drives the egocentric individual. And when we allow fresh understanding to underpin our actions we can begin to develop creative and innovative ways to tackle long standing problems.

We cannot change another person's personality, but we can influence their behaviour. And we do have the power to change ourselves. We each have the capacity to change our mindset and our actions. By understanding our colleague differently we might shift our perception which in turn could bring about a reduction in our stress levels. By trying out new behaviours we might over time cause our colleague to respond differently and feel less of a need to defend himself – which is after all – at the root of most ego-driven behaviour.

MANAGING EGO-ENERGY

Ego-energy is the force that drives us forward. It enables us to meet our personal, professional and emotional needs. It's what drives us to achieve great things, to express ourselves and to assert ourselves. But when it operates from a basis of low self-awareness and low self-esteem it will drive us to achieve at any cost, regardless of the harm we may be causing to the people around us and the environment in which we operate or the targets we are seeking to meet.

Managing our own ego-energy is one thing. Managing ego-energy in others requires insight, patience and wisdom. It can be difficult, frustrating and equally exciting and rewarding. In managing the ego-energy in others you are potentially offering them an opportunity to raise their self-awareness and their self-esteem. You are encouraging them to achieve great things and at the same time creating an environment in which they can experiment, stretch their boundaries and get out of their comfort zones, always knowing that they are

- safe – physically and emotionally
- visible – they are seen and acknowledged
- powerful – they are afforded *appropriate* status, recognition and autonomy

In managing the ego-energy of another individual you are helping him to meet his needs *and* find a way of operating that is right for his context. You are helping him to find creative and appropriate ways to achieve his personal and professional goals without needing to resort to some of the ego-defensive, inauthentic behaviours that often manifest in the egocentric individual.

RIGHTS AND RESPONSIBILITIES

It isn't just managers and leaders who have rights and responsibilities in the management of ego-energy in others. As a colleague and as an employee you may find yourself working alongside a colleague, or indeed a boss who is driven by her ego needs. You may find yourself caught up in the turmoil that egocentricity creates. You may be struggling to find ways to handle the relationship and your part in it. But you have a right to be treated with respect and to be heard by those you work with and those who manage you. And with that right goes a responsibility to be clear in articulating your standards, your boundaries and your expectations.

As a manager or a leader you have a right to expect good standards of performance, appropriate behaviour and proper utilisation of resources. You also have a responsibility to articulate those standards clearly and to give feedback on behaviour that you deem to be inappropriate. You have a responsibility to provide opportunities for stretching, fulfilling and satisfying work that will allow all individuals the opportunity to meet their ego needs safely and appropriately.

Managing and mobilising ego-energy effectively in those around you is essentially about paying attention to their self-awareness and self-esteem. Ultimate responsibility for each of these areas lies with the individual, but you as colleague, manager or leader can have a powerful impact.

7

CREATING AN EGO-FREE CULTURE

USE IT OR LOSE IT

Working in an ego-driven environment can deliver a quick fix of motivation and energy, but the longer-term impact can be physical exhaustion and emotional burn out. How do you create a culture that is free from the tyranny of the ego, yet at the same time allows ego needs to be acknowledged and met? A culture in which individual needs for power, status and recognition are used well and support the delivery of corporate goals? How do you make sure the energy the ego provides does not drain away from your business?

EGOS DRIVEN UNDERGROUND

There are cultures that are overtly ego-driven and those that are covertly ego-driven. There are those in which you will notice the obvious signs and symptoms: the strutting, preening and posturing. And there are those in which ego needs are so deeply hidden, so robustly denied, that you spot their manifestations only with a very watchful eye. In these systems you won't see the raw aggression of the overtly egotistical culture, but you will see degrees of subterfuge, manipulation, almost an infiltration by stealth of egos that aren't allowed a voice but will gain prominence and recognition despite the cultural norms that keep them suppressed. Because that's what egos do. They get their needs met.

THE ANGLICAN CHURCH HAS SOME BIG ONES GOING TO WASTE

The Anglican Church is an example of a system that wastes the ego-energy of the individuals within it. Egos that operate with stealth and caution to get their needs met in a culture that, like the voluntary sector, prides itself on its ethos of altruism. In the Anglican Church it is most definitely not OK for priests to seek prominence or be overtly ambitious. Priestly ministry, we are told, flourishes best when it is invisible, when it is not noticed. Because good ministry is about others. It is about putting others before yourself. It is about placing others centre stage and acting as a catalyst for their learning, growth and development. At weddings and funerals the good priest is a facilitator of others' joy and sorrow, but must never be the focus of attention. Individual needs for power status and recognition are unimportant. People are treated with respect and dignity and there is a place for everyone regardless of age, race or gender.

These are the espoused norms or rules that the Anglican Church hopes most of its priestly incumbents will seek to live out. It expects its clergymen and women to be egoless. And yet it recruits men and women with outstanding intellectual ability, with vision, drive and ambition who are keen to further not only the aims of the church, but also, dare it be said, their own.

The Anglican Church doesn't do ambition well. Ambition is one of the great unmentionables. In parishes throughout the country there are intelligent, visionary incumbents whose talents and energy are wasted because it's somehow not nice to use them to full effect. All at a time when the church is in decline and attendance figures are falling.

Recently a bishop was giving a closing address to 250 clergymen and women at a diocesan conference. He raised the topic of ambition. You could hear the temperature drop in the room. He said there is one thing worse than clergy who think they ought to be bishops. And that's clergy who think they ought to *have been* bishops. There was a stunned silence. Most of those in the hall would have fallen into one or other category but no-one had publicly acknowledged the presence of this ego-driven, shadow-side phenomena that was eating away at the very fabric of the church. This bishop had dared to say what shouldn't be said. He had blown the church's cover. He had lifted the lid on human frailty and imperfection. But, perhaps more importantly, he had dared to expose a shameful waste of human energy and enthusiasm within a struggling system that could ill afford to spare it.

In this system where does the ambition go? How are ego needs met? How do bright, capable priests meet their needs for power, status and recognition in ways that serve not just their own interests but those of the Church they work for and the people they serve? Many of those I spoke to were open about their desire to rise through the ecclesiastical hierarchy, but recognised a need to play down their ambitions, at least within church circles. Their way forward wasn't about looking at the selection criteria for jobs at the next level (there are no such clearly articulated criteria) and working towards meeting them. They all spoke of a widespread tendency towards putting yourself about, being seen in the right places and becoming active on the more prestigious national committees. All in the hope that someone with power and influence will spot your abilities and potential and beckon you towards greater things. You could argue that this is fairly innocuous behaviour and does no-one very much harm. But operating with stealth and caution takes energy. Energy that could be put to much better use.

If the Anglican Church did more to acknowledge and utilise the ego needs of its priestly incumbents it might be more dynamic, responsive and credible than it is today.

GIVING EGO NEEDS AN APPROPRIATE OUTLET

So how do you create a culture in which egos find an appropriate outlet?

Jonathan, a highly respected and experienced senior police chief, has been addressing the question of how to meet the ego needs of his officers for many years. Police forces across the UK, he explains, now attract highly motivated and capable individuals, a large proportion of whom enter the service keen to make an impact and secure promotion. Traditionally their needs for power, status and recognition have been met by moving up through the ranks, but competition is tough and there is an increasing proportion of officers willing and able to take on more responsibility. These men and women are proud to wear the uniform and be part of the police service. They have something to prove. But if this energy isn't managed appropriately difficulties arise as they seek not just to do their job well, but do it to prove a point – get noticed – often to the detriment of the public and their colleagues.

Jonathan believes that one way to address the dilemma is through empowerment; a concept that doesn't always sit well within a traditionally hierarchical, rank-based structure. In recent years has there been a sea change in attitudes in the police towards empowering constables and sergeants. Until five years ago they were still told what to do. The constable would say "I'll do it when the sergeant tells me to do it". Now attitudes and practices are changing and the potential emerging from the lower ranks is beginning to be recognised and utilised in ways that are not just about promotion.

One initiative that has had a profound and positive impact on the communities it was seeking to help has had a lasting effect on the young, capable constables involved. Communities First was set up two years ago to tackle crime and disorder in some of the most deprived, crime affected areas in the UK. Teams comprising a sergeant and four constables were tasked to go out to work with local communities in these areas and empower them to tackle some of their own challenges. These young and relatively inexperienced officers had to get out and build relationships of trust with people who had hitherto been hostile and deeply suspicious towards the police. They had to do more than simply "take out the criminals". They were tasked with empowering communities to identify their own problems and find solutions.

The chief officer overseeing the scheme knew that without experiencing empowerment for themselves these teams would never be able to empower the communities they were working with. "We gave these officers very little direction" he explains. "We gave them resources and support and I made sure I was available to them when they needed a sounding board. But essentially they were in charge. These officers went out into communities and did things they knew they were good at and things they didn't know they could do. They tackled crime. They knew they were good at that. But they also spent time talking and listening, gauging public opinion. They encouraged people to think about their environment and set their own standards. They supported these communities to be self-policing in a way that was unfamiliar and challenging". Over time the constables reported back that what they were seeking to do was beginning to work. They were proud to be part of an innovative and successful initiative. They earned respect and recognition from colleagues and the community. They experienced autonomy. They felt powerful. Their self-esteem had risen and their self-awareness had increased beyond all expectation. Their ego needs had been given an appropriate outlet.

LIBERATION FROM CULTURAL CONSTRAINTS

The Communities First initiative in many ways flew in the face of police tradition. In a small but significant way it dismantled parts of the police culture, causing officers to re-evaluate their performance, their potential and their motivation. These officers were being asked to take personal risks, get out of their comfort zones and operate in an unfamiliar way, requiring more self-reliance and willingness to learn than they had ever experienced. They were being asked to work collaboratively with each other without reliance on rank or seniority. They were being asked to work collaboratively with the public without playing the police card at the earliest sign of trouble. They were being asked to work with greater insight and self-awareness than had ever been expected of them before.

This initiative wasn't about them. It was about the communities they were serving. But by being liberated from familiar cultural constraints they were able to do a professional, worthwhile job *and* meet their own ego needs appropriately.

An initiative on this scale does not in itself change the culture of a vast and complex organisation. But it does begin to turn the tide and can show what is possible, even in the most traditional, ego-driven environment.

QUESTIONS TO BE ASKED

- in what ways are egos given an appropriate outlet in your organisation?
- how does the culture in your business stifle or liberate ego-energy?
- What are you going to do about it?

WCL – CREATING AN EGO-FREE CULTURE (AND REAPING BUSINESS BENEFITS)

In an ego-free culture ego needs are acknowledged and met in ways that further the aims of both the business *and* the individual. One notable example of a business that is explicitly setting out to create such a culture is WCL.

WCL is a relative newcomer to the change management consultancy arena. Established three years ago by three energetic and capable men with a Big Five consultancy background, WCL consciously set out to operate with what it describes as "ego-free values". And their ethos and philosophy appear to be working. They are now thirty-strong and expanding. Their client base has grown rapidly. And feedback from clients suggests they like what they're getting.

So what sets WCL apart from its competitors? Why has this initially small enterprise experienced such phenomenal growth? How has it come to share a stage with the big players?

THE WCL ETHOS: CONFIDENCE NOT ARROGANCE

Nigel, one of the founders of the business, believes WCL's success is a direct result of the culture he and his two fellow directors consciously and explicitly set out to create. From the beginning they ran workshops with employees to discuss values and beliefs. They felt it was important to involve everyone to ensure that the culture they were creating reflected everyone's views. "The ethos is discussed and explicit and it's largely about treating people well whether they be employees or clients. We recruit bright capable people but we believe in confidence not arrogance. That runs through everything we do".

The way WCL treats its consultants

Consultants joining the business know they won't have to wade through layers of hierarchy and bureaucracy to get to "the men at the top". In this consultancy the men at the top see themselves as the men in the centre of things. They are part of the team. They don't sit above it. Nigel explains: "the lack of hierarchy supports the way WCL works. Everyone in the company has access to the three directors whenever they want it. We consciously make time for them, whether it's to help them with a problem or to work with them on a specific job. If *they* want to manage *us* on a specific project they are leading that's fine. We treat our consultants as adults. We support them in managing their own budgets and case loads. Having to wade through several layers of hierarchy to get sign off for a million pound project is disempowering. We don't believe we're the experts and they are the novices. Our philosophy is 'let's work together and make this happen'".

"The thing about working at WCL is you don't have to operate as a different person when you come into the office. There's an integrity and authenticity about the way we work. We like to think there's less of a split between work and home persona. We want people to be themselves".

What sort of person?

You do have to be a certain sort of person to work for WCL. Ego-driven, brutally competitive applicants need not apply. "We are clear about our ethos and our culture and we share that early on in the recruitment process with potential applicants. We involve existing staff in the selection process to ensure a good fit with the business. The people who join us are professional and ambitious but we don't recruit people who want to succeed at the expense of those around them. We want people who are interested in their own development, who have the energy and drive to learn. Career development at WCL is not traditional. It's very much about personal development within the context of the business. Every year we allocate everyone a specific training budget and it's up to them how they spend it. All we ask is that they bring their learning back to the workplace and demonstrate how they are using it. It can be anything. It might be selling in Chinese. The appraisal system also starts with the individual and works back to the business. We ask people what they want to get out of the next year and how that impacts on what the company is trying to achieve. It's a different start point from most appraisal systems. We *all* have 360 degree feedback and people genuinely value the feedback they are given. It's not just a paper exercise. It works".

Everyone should be famous for something

Nigel believes one of the reasons WCL attracts young dynamic consultants is that it doesn't pigeon-hole them or try to box them in. People don't get stuck with a particular client base or a particular way of working just because they have initially shown themselves to do well in that area. They are encouraged to find their feet with different clients and new methods.

Nigel and his colleagues at WCL don't set out to encourage specialisms. Instead they foster the idea that everyone should be famous for something. "This is directly about meeting ego needs" Nigel says. "We encourage people to be innovative, to come up with new ideas. And we support them in putting those ideas into action".

Impact on the client

How does WCL's culture impact on the client? Nigel says he and his consultants work hard and work effectively. But he and his fellow directors don't encourage workaholism. They are clear that they expect their people to put in long hours when needed, but presenteeism for its own sake is discouraged. "Just being there doesn't mean you're adding value" he believes. "Sometimes clients expect you to work extraordinarily long hours because that's what they believe good consultants do. We talk to the client about the way we work. We put a lot of emphasis on building good client relationships. We work *with* them. We don't go in and do things *to* them. The adult relationships we foster in our own company are echoed in our dealings with the client. So far it seems to be working. Clients are staying with us and coming back for more. And that's good for business".

DIMENSIONS OF AN EGO-FREE CULTURE

How do you know whether you are working in an ego-free culture? What signs and symptoms tell the tale?

- everyone can be famous for something
- ego-energy is used, not wasted
- people work effectively, not just for effect
- workaholism is seen as unhealthy and unnecessary
- cross-fertilisation of ideas is the norm
- people have a voice regardless of rank or grade
- the "characters" don't hog all the space
- leadership is everywhere
- there is authentic, robust debate
- everyone is treated as an adult – there are few parent-child relationships
- leaders encourage autonomy rather than dependency
- relationships are respectful not sycophantic
- people know it's not about them – but they acknowledge what's in it for them
- confidence replaces arrogance
- empowerment replaces fear
- people are heard
- innovation is everywhere
- there is high self-esteem
- people can say "I don't know"
- you don't always have to get it right
- empires are unnecessary
- people don't have to hide and pretend
- collaboration replaces aggressive competition
- individuals take appropriate risks
- people are not afraid of being exposed
- emotional intelligence is given as much credence as intellectual ability
- individuals are not boxed in by job title
- people say what they think – with care and integrity
- learning replaces blame
- personal development is valued alongside professional development
- abusive relationships are identified and challenged
- charisma carries a health warning

YOUR RESPONSIBILITY

Whether you are the CEO, a senior manager or a front-line operator, what you do, your day-to-day interactions with people, your beliefs, your values and your attitudes all help shape the culture of your business and your immediate working environment. It is your responsibility to identify and challenge the hidden cultural norms that contaminate the culture of your business or your department. It is your responsibility to think about your own ego needs and how you meet them, responsibly, ethically and appropriately within the context of your organisation. It is your responsibility to weigh up the costs and benefits of the culture as it exists in your working environment. Does anything need to change? How? Why? What do you want instead?

An organisation's culture develops over time. Often the culture as it is now reflects things as they *were* rather than current realities. Perhaps your business has outgrown its culture. Perhaps it could risk doing things differently. Maybe its unspoken rules and norms no longer serve it well.

Moving from an ego-driven to an ego-free culture is not something to be done overnight. Culture change requires time, energy and resources. The investment can be high. But the costs of doing nothing may be higher.

FURTHER READING

Chained to The Desk: A Guidebook for Workaholics, Their Partners and Children and the Clinicians who Treat Them
Bryan E Robinson PhD
1998 New York University Press New York
ISBN 0-8147-7556-X

Growing Leaders
Steve Yearout and Gerry Miles
2001 ASTD US
ISBN 1-56286-289-8

Leadership
Rudolph W Giuliani & Ken Kurson
2002 Little, Brown London
ISBN 0 316 86101 4

Level 5 Leadership
Jim Collins
January 2001
Harvard Business Review

Managing Ego-Energy
Ralph H Kilmann, Ines Kilmann and Associates
1994 Jossey-Bass Inc California
ISBN 1-55542-618-2

Meeting The Shadow
Jeremiah Abrams and Connie Zweig
1991 Penguin Putnam Inc New York
ISBN 0-87477-618-X

Narcissistic Leaders: The Incredible Pros, the Inevitable Cons
Michael Maccoby
January 2000
Harvard Business Review

Owning Your Own Shadow
Robert A Johnson
1993 Harper Collins New York
ISBN 0-06-250754-0

Personality Theories
Larry A Hjelle and Daniel J Ziegler
1992 McGraw Hill Singapore
ISBN 0-07-029079-2

The Ego and the Id
Sigmund Freud. Translated by James Strachey
1960 WW Norton & Co Inc New York
ISBN 0-393-00142-3

The Harder they Fall
Roderick M. Kramer
October 2003
Harvard Business Review

The New Leaders
Daniel Goleman, Richard Boyatzis and Annie Mckee
2002 Little, Brown London
ISBN 0-316-85765-3

Why Should Anyone be Led by You?

Robert Goffee and Gareth Jones

September 2000

Harvard Business Review

Working the Shadow Side

Gerard Egan

1994 Jossey-Bass California

ISBN 0-7879-0011-7

SUSAN DEBNAM

Susan Debnam is an independent executive coach, working with leaders across private, public and voluntary sector organisations. A partner in Debnam Booth, she has fifteen years' experience in the field of leadership development.

Susan is currently working with the Cabinet Office coaching senior figures in the police, universities and a range of government departments. Voluntary activity includes giving professional time to Chase Children's Hospice. Susan has an MSc in Organisational Change and maintains an on-going interest in the creation of energising and nurturing work environments.

Susan lives in Guildford with her husband and business partner, Joe Booth and her young daughter. When she is not working she enjoys seeing her friends and running along the river.

THE TRUTH ABOUT BUSINESS

Mine's Bigger Than Yours is part of The Truth About Business series which tackles some of the most pertinent and sensitive topics in business and work today. The series is edited by Sally Bibb.

Other titles in the series are:

The Stone Age Company
Why the companies we work for are dying and how they can be saved
Sally Bibb

Just for the Money?
What really motivates us at work
Adrian Furnham with Tom Booth

Why Your Boss is Programmed to be a Dictator
A book for anyone who has a boss or is a boss
Chetan Dhruve

The Stone Age Company
Why the companies we work for are dying and
how they can be saved
Sally Bibb

**Companies need to change: they are outdated and ineffective in
the way they are run and they are losing out in the increasingly
competitive world of business.**

That's the view of Sally Bibb, author of this thought-provoking and
controversial book, which challenges leaders to think about their
organizations and how they should be managed.

The Stone Age company is an uninspiring place to work – it is an
organization that has practices that don't work anymore. It talks
the talk but doesn't walk the walk. It is characterized by hierarchy,
controlling management techniques, managerial bad behavior and
spin. Is your company like this?

This book is a wake-up call. It will inspire leaders to reinvent
the way businesses are run, encouraging them to turn their
organization into a different type of company: a company that
thrills its customers, is innovative and efficient, is fun and
energizing to work for. Using examples of successful organizations
including the Innocent Drinks company, WL Gore, Timberland and
Southwest Airlines, and her own personal experiences, Bibb shows
what innovative companies do and how they do it.

Written in a clear and inspirational way, unlike traditional
management books, *The Stone Age Company* is a book that all
managers, leaders, employees, and shareholders should buy if
they want to succeed in today's fast-changing business world.

ISBN-10 1-904879-43-8
ISBN-13 978-1-904879-43-5

UK £9.99 / USA $18.95 / CAN $25.95

Just for the Money?
What really motivates us at work
Adrian Furnham with Tom Booth

How many people work just for the money? What is your time actually worth? How does your organization handle the trade-off between the good, the cheap and the fast?

These are some of the questions asked by Adrian Furnham and Tom Booth, the authors of this thought-provoking book. *Just for the Money?* challenges our assumptions about money in the workplace, at home and in our daily lives.

The book is predicated on four fundamental, evidence-based truths: most people are far from rational with respect to money; our attitudes to beliefs about our spending and saving of money have much to do with our childhood and early education; at work, money is a powerful demotivator, rather than a powerful motivator; and money and well-being are only tangentially related.

Furnham and Booth explore money and motivation at work, money beliefs, money in society, money and religion, the meaning of money, the importance of money, money as a motivator or demotivator, money and emotions, and money and family. *Just for the Money?* even includes useful tips for helping your children to understand about money and teaching them to be sensible with it.

Unlike traditional business guides, this fascinating book is one that you must buy if you are interested in money!

ISBN-10 1-904879-50-0
ISBN-13 978-1-904879-50-3

UK £9.99 / USA $18.95 / CAN $25.95

Why Your Boss is Programmed to be a Dictator
A book for anyone who has a boss or is a boss
Chetan Dhruve

A book that offers a completely different way of looking at the issue of boss behaviour.

The vast majority of people have suffered under a bad boss at some stage in their careers. The office becomes a daily living hell. But the biggest tragedy is that even if you quit and move to another job, there is no guarantee you will end up with a decent boss. In fact, the chances are, the new boss will exhibit the same dictatorial characteristics.

This book examines why bosses behave the way they do. When you get a new boss, you are simply told, "John will be your manager." John now has power over you. And because bosses are not elected, they begin to display the tendencies of a dictator. Moreover, as a subordinate, you will also begin to behave like a subject in a dictatorship. The author argues that this dictatorial system within the majority of companies is the root cause of problematic workplace behaviour. By understanding this, both employees and bosses can take the first steps to creating a better relationship.

ISBN-10 0-462-09902-4
ISBN-13 978-0-462-09902-6

UK £8.99 / USA $14.95 / CAN $20.95